Youth

in the Community of Disciples

D0112142

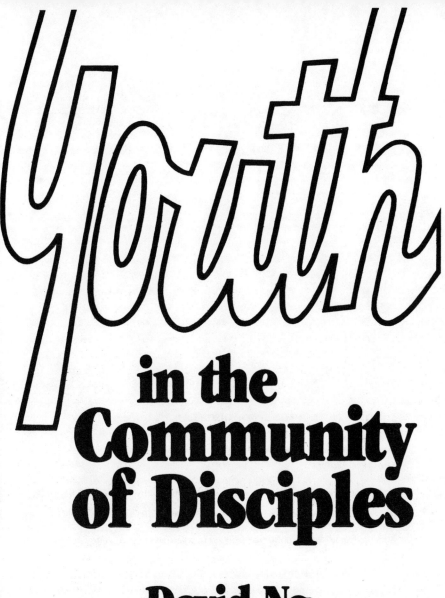

Youth

in the
Community
of Disciples

David Ng

Judson Press ® Valley Forge

YOUTH IN THE COMMUNITY OF DISCIPLES

Copyright © 1984
Judson Press, Valley Forge, PA 19482-0851

Second Printing, 1984

All rights reserved. No part of this publication may be reproduced, stored in a retrieval system, or transmitted in any form or by any means, electronic, mechanical, photocopying, recording, or otherwise, without the prior permission of the copyright owner, except for brief quotations included in a review of the book.

Bible quotations are from the Revised Standard Version of the Bible copyrighted 1946, 1952 © 1971, 1973 by the Division of Christian Education of the National Council of the Churches of Christ in the U.S.A., and used by permission.

Library of Congress Cataloging in Publication Data

Ng, David.
  Youth in the community of disciples.

  Includes bibliographical references.
  1. Church work with youth.   2. Youth—Religious life.
I. Title.
BV4447.N45   1984   259'.2   83-19977
ISBN 0-8170-1015-7

The name JUDSON PRESS is registered as a trademark in the U.S. Patent Office.
Printed in the U.S.A.

Dedicated to Dick Wichman,
whose lifelong ministry with the youth
of Chinatown, San Francisco,
is the basis for this book.

Foreword

In January, 1983, a group of persons with a deep concern for ministry with youth gathered at the American Baptist Assembly, Green Lake, Wisconsin. The event which brought them there was Creation 3, the third in a series of conferences for youth ministry professionals sponsored by the Department of Ministry with Youth of the American Baptist Board of Educational Ministries.

That group was privileged to hear the lectures upon which this book is based. It was a challenging experience because in the lectures David Ng issued a call to think deeply about the ultimate issues of youth ministry. That call had the effect of refocusing the attention of those who were there on something they knew already—that the ultimate purpose of youth ministry is the development of disciples of Jesus Christ who live out their commitment to Christ in their daily lives. We knew that already, but Dave's presentation of that message brought new insights and enthusiasm to all of us.

So often in our concern for the involvement of youth in the

church's youth program we fall into the trap of entertaining them, of making things easy for them. Youth ministry all too frequently ends up as something that adults do for (or to) the youth. In our concern for youth, we sometimes forget that we also have a commitment to the gospel. That commitment challenges us to share the entire gospel message with youth. Youth ministry must challenge as well as entertain, it must question as well as affirm, it must call forth as well as accept. It cannot be merely ministry *to* youth which focuses exclusively on responding to the needs of youth, but must always be ministry *with* youth, which calls youth to join with adults in ministering to each other and the world. That is what discipleship is all about.

It is our hope in sharing these lectures through this book that you, too, will be challenged to think deeply about youth ministry and will find inspiration for a continuing commitment to ministry with youth.

Jeffery D. Jones, Director
Department of Ministry with Youth
American Baptist Churches, USA

Contents

Preface

For a number of years the Department of Ministry with Youth, American Baptist Churches, USA has conducted a training and renewal conference for leaders involved in youth ministry. It was my privilege to present to the group gathered as "Creation 3" my views of how youth ministry can become vital. The participants were active workers in congregations and regional educational networks. They received my views graciously and offered responses thoughtfully. Dealing with matters of importance to the church, we were seeking to be more faithful and capable ministers with young persons.

From the beginning, when the planners of Creation 3 extended the invitation and made preparations for the conference, they agreed it would not be necessary to present "the latest thing in youth ministry." The planners intended to go back to basics and to rediscover or reinvent youth ministry. In a field of church work which is highly susceptible to fads and gimmicks, the planners chose to reiterate some core concepts of the Christian gospel. They wanted to restore youth ministry to its central purposes defined in biblical and theological terms. *Youth in the Community of Disciples* is an attempt to state certain central purposes of youth ministry. This book seeks to establish a theological foundation on which psychological, sociological, and educational components can rest, to form a whole, balanced ministry with youth. The insights of Dietrich Bonhoeffer, particularly, are used as a theological foundation.

The first chapter of the book reaches to the heart of youth ministry, advocating the call to discipleship and mission as the focus of the church's work. In chapter 2 the natural, necessary task of identity formation is put into a theological framework of faith pilgrimage. Personal identity is defined in relationship to the humanity of Jesus and to Christian identity. Young people want to belong to a community. This desire is discussed in chapter 3 in the light of Bonhoeffer's radical and demanding perceptions of *koinonia* or Christian community. The final chapter suggests how adults can become servant leaders ministering to young people.

The youth ministry team of the American Baptist Churches, Jeffrey Jones, Marilyn Marston, and Donald Ng, helped give shape to this book. They gave an old hand in youth ministry an opportunity to put together his thirty and more years of experience, ideas, and dreams. These understandings of youth ministry have been learned from countless colleagues—brothers and sisters in the community of disciples. They are too numerous to name here but their witness is evident and appreciated. Special thanks go to my wife, Irene, for her thoughtful questions and expert help, and to my sons, Steve and Andy, for all they have taught me.

David Ng
Brooklyn, 1983

Taking Up the Cross

You care about young people. You also care about the gospel of Jesus Christ. You care about the church and about how young persons can be a part of the church, contributing to it, learning from it, and responding to its proclamation of the gospel.

I have been involved in youth ministry for over thirty years, as a young participant, leader, curriculum developer, program designer, teacher, and parent of two young persons. I, too, care about young people, the gospel, and the church.

You and I share a concern for young people and a desire that they find themselves and their places within the church and in the full reaches of life, relationships, work, and personal fulfillment. This book speaks to these concerns and desires. It speaks of a ministry with youth which focuses on helping young people to hear the challenging call of Jesus Christ to discipleship, community, and service, and to find their identities through the process of responding to that call.

We in the church do not always make it easy for young people to hear the call to discipleship or to respond to it. I recall experiencing a sense of exasperation, almost of despair, during a workshop for adult leaders of youth. The workshop was well organized, provided solid content and good group processes. Things were moving along very nicely. Toward the end an adult leader spoke, "In our senior high group we have a clique of four girls. They have a great influence on the group. But they won't come unless their friends come, and they won't come unless it's fun. The parents of our kids tell us we need to put on attractive programs because they don't want their children dropping out of the church. What should we do?"

My grimace turned to a weak smile as I answered, "Quit the fun and games. Install a very demanding youth ministry program centering on service and work projects. If the girls don't want to come, tell them they can go to . . . ."

There was a good laugh; the workshop got finished; and I flew back home. Workshop leaders can do that; they can say outrageous things, then leave town. Shortly after that incident my wife, Irene, and I were called to a special meeting in the church our family had recently joined. The parents of the junior high young people were called together to discuss what to do about the junior high youth fellowship which was on the verge of falling apart. We parents agreed that we would need to back up the volunteer leaders. Most parents had little experience in youth ministry but we needed to support those who were trying to do it. We needed better programs that were more interesting and more fun. Kids don't want to come to a dull youth fellowship.

Irene and I felt both anger and tears as we drove home from the meeting that night.

The image of youth ministry perceived by the parents and pastor was 10,000 light years removed from that with which Irene and I had grown up and from what we felt should be the emphasis. We had grown up in a church that made great demands on its young people. Belonging to that church meant, for a young person, giving up a lot and taking on a lot. Irene and I felt that our sons, Andy and Steve, did not need any more entertainment—they had plenty of that done in good fashion by the school, community, friends, and home. We wanted Andy and Steve to be encountered by Jesus Christ, and to experience what it means to be faithful members of the church of Jesus Christ. That is why we felt both anger and tears.

Our story is not unique. Perhaps your story is different and you have much better news to report regarding the state of youth ministry in our churches. But chances are that you have experienced situations similar to the two just described. When doing youth ministry, churches often strive for wrong goals using wrong methods.

Among the wrong goals are those of maintenance, fellowship, and protection. The goal of *maintenance* is to keep the young people coming to the church. Do whatever you have to do to keep them coming. Food, games, the promise of being in the right crowd, the winning personalities of the leaders, attractive facilities, and exotic trips are some of the ploys used to maintain good attendance. There are as many ploys as there are leaders' manuals promising success with youth.

The goal of *fellowship* is to help the young people who come to the church to be happy with one another and to get along together. "Body building" exercises and other dynamic group processes are employed to engender good group spirit. Conflicts are played down, as are diversities and differences. The youth fellowship is molded into one happy group.

The goal of *protection* is to indoctrinate the young people, or inoculate them, so that they will not fall prey to cults, drugs, and other civil perversions.

The problem of seeking the wrong goals is followed by using the wrong methods. A popular but wrong method is that of *entertaining* the young people. Adults in the church believe, or are led by the young people to believe, that when activities are fun and entertaining, young people will attend. Not every church will have as elaborate a setup as was found in a certain independent youth evangelism program, in which a young person would be called and then seated at a chair on stage and asked "Truth or Consequences" type questions. The consequence, which generated much laughter from the youth audience, was a mild electrical shock when the wrong answer was given by the hapless victim. Most churches are not that crude. But great is the number of churches who believe that unless they have a guitar-playing, song-leading leader, they will not be able to attract young people and hold them.

Some methods, while not necessarily wrong, reflect an *unrealistic approach* to working with young people. Adults who work with youth can operate from a sense that adolescence is pathological, like an illness to be overcome.[1] Certainly there are not many adults in the church who wish to be exposed for long periods of time to adolescents. In their negative manifestations, adult attitudes toward the alleged pathology of adolescence presuppose that people in the teen years behave irrationally, irresponsibly, and erratically. Teens cannot be trusted or depended upon. They are predictable only in the sense that they are sure to get in trouble.

Applied more benevolently, the adult attitude toward adolescents is that they are in a time of transition and therefore can be expected to be inconsistent and self-centered. While no longer children, the adolescents are not yet adults; they are not yet "real" people, and no lasting accomplishments can be expected from these people who are in a stage of transition. Youth ministry, in this light, is a time for playing, for marking time, and for holding on to the young people. They are put "on hold" until they can grow up.

A related and equally unrealistic method for working with young people is to lead them on the basis of *what adults believe young persons really are and really want*. However, the times change. Adults, who did go through genuine experiences of adolescence themselves, change. Their values have an additional ten, twenty, or thirty years of tempering. Even well-informed adults who are familiar with the best works of psychology and sociology, will not be able to know the mind of an adolescent without asking that adolescent. There is no way to do youth ministry without youth involvement in planning.

Furthermore, ministering with young people through psychological analysis, while not wrong in itself, may be a method that is incomplete. Many persons, such as myself, who have conducted workshops and written articles on how to understand and work with young people, are guilty of this overemphasis on psychological analysis. It may be true that adults need to know what is happening with persons during their adolescent years. Too often, however, adult leaders think of adolescent development only in terms of individual psychological development. For many of us there is a mystique about the solitary adolescent who is experiencing a lonely, even heroic, journey through a difficult time in life. But a youth ministry that focuses on helping an individual young person fulfill individual personal identity runs the risk of shaping the young members of the church into individualistic, self-centered Christians—which is a contradiction in terms.

One more wrong method must be pointed out. In some churches the youth program is conducted on the basis of *impersonal relationships*. On the surface there may be activities that bring young people together and help them to relate to one other. Looking beneath the surface, however, we find that the young people do not become genuine friends. The youth fellowship or Sunday church school class is where persons from different high schools get together several hours a week to do a few things together. But they do not become the kind of friends who really know and care about one another, and give of themselves to one another. Among the members of the group, youth and adults alike, there is tolerance of one another and an easy camaraderie. But there is no real *grace*. There is no forgiveness, no community; there is only cheap grace.

I am convinced that youth ministry must move away from condescension, unreality, impersonal relationships, and individualism. Our task is to rediscover or to reinvent youth ministry.

Some Help for Our Task

Rediscovering or reinventing youth ministry is no easy task. There are no simple answers. One resolve needs to be made at the outset: develop an impregnable immunity to any resource for youth ministry which displays the word "success." "Successful Youth Programs," "1001 Successful Icebreakers," "Successful Ways to Win Youth," and their ilk are to be avoided. Some other suggestions for doing youth ministry follow.

1. Listen to all the parties involved.

When engaging in youth ministry, consult with everyone who is involved and has a stake in how the church does its youth ministry. Listen with sympathy and empathy to learn what goals the church has set for its ministry with youth. Also, listen with a healthy grain of salt! Pastors and church leaders may have key perspectives on the church's goals in overall ministry and in the goals for youth ministry. However, they may also be defensive because the youth program is not succeeding (again, be careful with that word).

Listen to parents. They really do care about their teenage children, so it is imperative to hear their concerns. Many parents are feeling very bad and are hurting in regard to their sons and daughters. As the saying goes: "Adolescence is an awkward age—for the parents." In my own case there was the poignancy of being a nationally known "expert" on youth ministry who, along with my wife, found ourselves frequently reverting to a four-letter word when it came to dealing with our own two teenage children: "Help!" Youth ministry leaders who can listen to the parents will find concerned allies and also an arena of ministry in itself, that of ministering with parents.

Effective youth ministry requires listening to the young people and involving them in the approach and program. The young people know their own inner beings, thoughts, and questions. We are dealing with their lives and their youth ministry. With their involvement, the goals and methods of youth ministry are more realistic and relevant. But even here, adult leaders need to listen with a healthy grain of salt or at least listen to young persons in a larger context than just that of their own lives and visions. Adolescents know what is inside them, but they are experiencing adolescence for the first time. They may not have the same long-range perspective of a grandmother or grandfather who has seen adolescence three times— in one's self, one's children, and one's grandchildren. Older persons can afford a more bemused look at adolescent behavior, knowing that "adolescence is serious but not fatal."

Workers with youth need to listen to the community of faith, too. More will be said about this in a later chapter on the importance of community in youth ministry.

2. Learn from research.

Research about young people and their subculture enhances rapport and relationships. Such research need not be limited to statistical reports and the grimly serious descriptions of adolescent behavior and societies, given in clinical or scientific form in books and journals. Some research on adolescence can be fun. We can look at and listen to youth culture on our own. Seeing movies about adolescents can be both enjoyable and instructive. While "exploitation films" such as the alleged horror movies can be avoided, were you to attend a showing of such a movie, it would be instructive to look behind the scenes for the inherent values expressed or the manner in which young persons are shown. Turning away from the screen to look at the audience may be very instructive! There are films of good quality which treat adolescents realistically and without condescension. In recent years these films have provided thought-provoking depictions of young people: *Ordinary People, Breaking Away, My Bodyguard, Tex, Gregory's Girl, The Chosen*. When adults see such movies with young persons, the consequent conversations about adolescence can be illuminating.

Music on records, discs, tapes, on the radio, and on television, portrays a world that is not easy for any adult over thirty to understand or appreciate. In this area there may be reluctance to reveal too much to an adult lest this domain of adolescence be breached. But when young persons are willing to try to explain their music, adults can begin to hear statements of aspirations, fears, values, and visions.

Watching television can take on new dimensions when an adult is looking for expressions of teenage values and ideals. Less important are the actual sitcom shows, comedy programs, and music. It is the response of the young persons which brings information and insight for the adult leader. From the way young people respond to television shows, in their speech, dress, metaphors, and images, one can discern values about sex roles, parental roles, how conflict is to be resolved, how authority is viewed, and so forth. And don't forget to watch the commercials.

More traditional forms of research are sources of information for adults who work with youth. Much of this research is in the field of psychology, particularly adolescent development. There are great values and also some pitfalls in learning about adolescent development. The same can be said of sociological research. As has been stated here, sociological samplings can be fun. More serious research has been done and is available to help adult leaders understand rites of passage, group behavior, cultural values, and the like. The next chapter will address the importance of learning from the psychology and sociology of adolescence.

3. Use a planning process.

Seeing a church using a good planning process in youth ministry is seeing one that is trying to get away from merely doing youth ministry as it has always been done, willy-nilly. A planning process requires an articulation of a rationale for youth ministry based on a sense of the needs and interests of the young people. Once the rationale is established, that is, the goals are stated, then appropriate structures, programs, and resources can be determined. Fortunately most denominations have published useful guides to planning in youth ministry. Every church can find a guide that will show how the planning process can be utilized.

4. Use group process skills.

Group skills are more than gimmicks, and leaders who work hard at developing such skills will find them extremely valuable. Youth ministry is not only the transmission of information about God and the church, it is also the sharing of faith and relationships. Superficially, being able to be a group is a necessary part of youth ministry. More profoundly, group skills can be used to enhance experiences of Christian community.

Chapters 4 and 5 on community and leadership will speak of this important topic.

5. Become well trained.

Anyone who has read this far into this book probably is already convinced of the importance of training for youth leadership. The need for training is undisputed. What constitutes good training is subject to debate and the final chapter in this book on leadership expresses one view.

Thus, in the five suggestions listed here a small accumulation of potential helps has been provided for the rediscovery of youth ministry. But you may be bored with such a list because it paves no new roads and likely deals with activities which are already well practiced by you. I, too, am impatient with this list. My "gut feeling," or personal conviction, is that the heart of youth ministry is somewhere else, somewhere other than in right knowledge or technique. For years now, many of us have been listening to the participants, learning from research, using a planning process, applying group skills, and obtaining training. All of this is helpful. However, one thing is needful. To renew youth ministry, the one thing needed is to rediscover *discipleship*.

Discipleship Is the Heart of Youth Ministry

The exasperation over the four girls who would not come to youth fellowship unless it was fun, was not directed toward the girls but showed an impatience with a church that failed to make clear to the girls the meaning of discipleship. Jesus Christ calls us to follow him. The anger and tears over the parents' meeting dealing with how to save a failing youth program was an expression of how much my wife and I wanted our two sons to hear the call of Jesus Christ and to be challenged to respond to it. The reason why youth programs that emphasize maintenance, fellowship, and protection are wrong is that these programs make it virtually impossible for young persons to be confronted by the demands of Jesus Christ to follow him. There may be at least twenty-four good reasons why we do youth ministry, but the primary reason is to present to young people the Good News of Jesus Christ, and the demands of Jesus Christ.

In this century one person who has presented this message about discipleship vividly and profoundly is Dietrich Bonhoeffer. Most, if not all of us, know that Bonhoeffer's life was itself a model of discipleship. He was a gifted theologian and teacher whose own understanding of discipleship led him to act against the Nazis in Germany. Imprisoned for his involvement in a plot to destroy Hitler, he nevertheless found it possible to write and to witness while in a prison cell. Eventually his discipleship led him to the gallows and martyrdom. The promise of Bonhoeffer, the great theological works, did not get written, for it was in midlife that Bonhoeffer was jailed and then hanged. But he did write several books which have called twentieth-century people back to a radical Christianity, one which is faithful to its roots. Perhaps the most influential of these books is *The Cost of Discipleship*.[2] This call to a renewed sense of commitment gave impetus to the church to take risks, to be faithful, and to live sacrificially and die in the name of Jesus Christ.

The hard and demanding words of *The Cost of Discipleship* are timely and significant for youth ministry today. Four of Bonhoeffer's points help us to rediscover what we must do in youth ministry.

1. We do not call ourselves; Jesus Christ calls us into discipleship.
2. The first step in discipleship is obedience.
3. Jesus Christ calls us to discipleship through the church.
4. Discipleship means following Jesus; following Jesus means the cross.

We do not call ourselves; Jesus Christ calls us into discipleship.

Bonhoeffer was concerned that too many church members were Christian in name only. They really were not disciples but persons who created their own definitions of the Christian faith and life. It was an easy life in which the Christian religion served the personal desires of the so-called believer. Similar dangers exist in youth ministry. Persons can go through a youth program, have a good time, learn a few Bible facts, and be led to think that this is what Christianity is about. Christianity is experienced as being soft, undemanding, and ultimately unfulfilling and unworthy of the young person's attention and commitment. Do we dare imagine a youth program that makes demands on young persons?

Is it possible to design a youth program that is tailored to the requirements of the gospel and of discipleship, rather than to the institutional requirements of the church, or the sentiments of the parents, or the preferences of the young people? What would youth ministry look like if its main focus were on discipleship?

A youth ministry reinvented to emphasize discipleship does not necessarily drop all the usual youth-oriented activities. Such a ministry will need programs and resources to help young persons to gain a sense of identity, to be able to relate to one another, and to grow in personhood. This means social and recreational activities and discussions that are interesting and stimulating. Examples of such activities abound: weekend retreats, going out for ice cream, studying the lives of men and women who have stood for justice and peace, and so forth. But the focus is sharpened. All is directed toward discipleship. Be it Bible study or basket weaving, every activity is an opportunity to present discipleship, to exemplify discipleship, and to equip young persons to be disciples. Youth ministry is to engage persons in discipleship.

The first step in discipleship is obedience.

One of Bonhoeffer's most famous points is that discipleship is not cheap grace; it is costly grace. The cost of discipleship is one's life. The cost is obedience to the sovereign Jesus Christ rather than to one's own desires and plans for life. Cheap grace is calling one's self into discipleship on one's own terms.

Young people are not necessarily to blame for wanting cheap grace. It may be the only variety they have been shown. They indulge in cheap-grace-type values and forms, as do so many parents and role models. Many young people are up to their ears in the "me-generation." They dress in $40 jeans, play with cars and video games, own numerous albums and cassettes, use makeup heavily, and spend their free time in self-indulgent exercises on the beach or at the shopping mall. These may be signs to some of us that our young people are heavy users of the "me-first approach." Yet the me-first approach may be an unconscious coverup for a nuclear disease. Could it be that our generation suffers from a mental and psychic illness in which the victim feels there is no real future, no hope, because sooner or later somebody will push the buttons of nuclear holocaust?[3]

The doctrine of cheap grace, being Christian the easy way, conveniently and "hassle-free," is a doctrine young people learn from their elders. There are not many adults providing good models of discipleship for the young people to emulate. There are even fewer churches where discipleship is preached and practiced so that young persons can see and understand what obedience really means.

One way obedience is acted upon is not to press for one's own claim but to accept the claims and to obey the demands of someone else—in this case the claims and demands of Jesus Christ. Obeying in this way is paradoxical, with a strange and seemingly opposite result. This kind of obedience results in freedom. It is a receiving of grace. To obey the call of Christ is to find a new life.

> Such grace is *costly* because it calls us to follow, and it is *grace* because it calls us to follow *Jesus Christ*. It is costly because it costs a man his life, and it is grace because it gives a man the only true life. It is costly because it condemns sin, and grace because it justifies the sinner. Above all, it is *costly* because it cost God the life of his Son: "ye were bought at a price," and what has cost God much cannot be cheap for us. Above all, it is *grace* because God did not reckon his Son too dear a price to pay for our life, but delivered Him up for us. Costly grace is the Incarnation of God.[4]

Jesus calls us to discipleship through the church.

This is a third learning for youth ministry from *The Cost of Discipleship*. This point was stated negatively earlier when there was the complaint that young people have inadequate models of discipleship and obedience today. To state the point positively, young people will hear the call to discipleship from their brothers and sisters who are disciples.

There are instances of persons who have responded to the call of Jesus Christ found in prayer, study, or perhaps in the reading of the Bible. That was not my experience, at least not in total. I heard the call of Jesus Christ because Wilmer Fong, Low Chan, Dick Wichman, Sunny Chan, and Lorna Logan called me to be a Christian. How many of us came to know and to follow Jesus by reading about him in a book? Most of us had discipleship communicated to us through persons. Faithful contemporary disciples and a faithful church were the means by which Jesus Christ spoke to us. Youth ministry must be the process by which one person calls another to faith and to discipleship.

Discipleship means following Jesus; following Jesus means the cross.

"When Christ calls a man he bids him come and die."[5] This is a very harsh saying. On second thought, in the context of youth ministry this is a very hopeful saying. To encounter Christ and to follow Christ is to abandon the attachments of the world and the old person. We give it all up and take on a new identity as disciples of Jesus Christ. For a young person this may be the best news she or he has ever heard.

From now on, therefore, we regard no one from a human point of view; even though we once regarded Christ from a human point of view, we regard him thus no longer. Therefore if any one is in Christ, [that one] is a new creation; the old has passed away, behold the new has come. All this is from God, who through Christ has reconciled us to [God's] self and gave us the ministry of reconciliation; that is, in Christ God was reconciling the world to [God's] self, not counting their trespasses against them, and entrusting to us the message of reconciliation. So we are ambassadors for Christ, God making [God's] appeal through us. We beseech you on behalf of Christ, be reconciled to God. For our sake [God] made [Christ] to be sin who knew no sin, so that in

[Christ] we might become the righteousness of God (2 Corinthians 5:16-21).

The good news for young people is this possibility of death to the old and birth to the new, so that they become new beings in Christ. The bad news is this: Following Jesus leads a person to the cross.

Discipleship may not lead to a cross or to a martyr's death. But for young persons as well as others, discipleship does lead to a style of living that requires sacrifice and often suffering. Growing up in Christian families in communities where church membership is common, many young persons may not realize the cost of discipleship and the sacrifices that may be demanded of those who would be faithful. The followers of Jesus Christ, if they are to be faithful to their calling, often will need to take stands against popular attitudes and activities or will need to take action against injustice and oppression. Just as one example, a Christian may feel that it is more faithful and proper to spend the first portion of one's earnings to provide money for humanitarian causes, rather than for one's own material benefit. For a teenager this may mean pledging some money to the church for mission causes rather than spending it for a fashionable sweater or the latest hit records. As such examples accumulate, it becomes obvious that the young disciple's values and priorities differ from those of the predominant peer culture. At a much more difficult level, a young person must work out what it means to be a Christian disciple in the nuclear age. While one's peers and the culture may be concentrating on "getting it while it can be got," the Christian may be called to a lean life-style and to costly peacemaking activities. While the majority resign themselves to an inevitable nuclear holocaust, the Christian is assigned to a position of hope, based on a belief in the resurrection and ultimate victory of God.

A disciple not only spends one's money differently, but also one's time, and more importantly, one's life, differently. J. B. Phillips characterizes this distinction vividly in his paraphrase of Romans 12:1-2:

With eyes wide open to the mercies of God, I beg you, my

brothers [and sisters], as an act of intelligent worship, to give him your bodies, as a living sacrifice, consecrated to him and acceptable by him. Don't let the world around you squeeze you into its own mold, but let God remold your minds from within, so that you may prove in practice that the plan of God for you is good, meets all his demands and moves toward the goal of true maturity.[6]

To be a disciple, a young Christian may have to give up some comfort or a circle of belonging. Each young disciple's sacrifice and suffering will be unique and personal. But the cross will be required, and the church must be honest and helpful in informing young persons that being Christian is costly.

Sacrifice and suffering may develop in more positive forms as discipleship is interpreted as a call to witness and service. A strong case could be made for defining youth ministry as *youth in mission*. Evangelism, witness, and service are forms of youth activity in such a ministry. A church will not "go far wrong" to have a program for youth consisting mostly of having the members doing things for others. Such a church may be willing to gamble that the aftermath of this type of programming is that the young persons will gain a sense of who they are and how they relate, and will see that in serving others, they have gained much for themselves.

An example of a mission orientation in youth ministry comes from the town of Old Greenwich, Connecticut. In the Presbyterian church there, most young persons participate in the confirmation program leading to full, responsible membership in the church. The leaders realized several years ago that the young people in this very affluent community may have studied about sacrifice and service, but still had no real notion of what these are. Service in Old Greenwich is what you get when you are in your room with your friends and you ring the bell to have the maid come up with sandwiches. So the confirmation process culminated in the participants signing a covenant or contract to engage in specific acts of service. Some signed up to do "candy striping" in hospitals, some to do tutoring, some to do house repairs for the elderly, and others to do similar acts of ministry for someone else. The volunteers met regularly to hear what one another did, to offer support, and to pray. These young persons began to understand themselves as servants.

Another example of mission orientation in youth ministry is practiced at an inner-city ethnic minority church in San Francisco. In that church there is a large youth program with several hundred persons participating in a variety of activities. There are social, recreational, educational, and religious activities virtually every day of the week and a dozen times on Sundays. Every young person who participates in the program is asked to do some form of service. In some cases a young visitor is invited for the first time, not to a party or an entertainment, but to help with a work project—perhaps scrubbing floors at the community center or delivering furniture to immigrant newcomers. Young adolescents are asked to do group projects, as befit their stage of development and interest. They are also asked to assume leadership for their own group, holding office and conducting their own meetings. As the participants get older, they are asked to do forms of service requiring more skills, responsibility, and self-giving. By the time the participant is a young adult, that person, in the name of Christ, has swept scores of club-room floors, washed dozens of cars and sent tens of dollars to humanitarian causes, taught church school classes for children, gone off in teams of four to help in summer programs in other churches, spent hours in the hot summer sun ministering to migrant farm workers and their families, and peeled buckets of potatoes or counseled cabins full of campers. Being a member of the youth program in this church entails one act of service after another. Youth ministry is youth-in-mission. To the point of over-emphasis, the clear message in this church is that Christianity involves mission.

One more example can illustrate what an emphasis on mission may mean. The church in Austin which had the parents' meeting to discuss how to save a failing junior high youth fellowship eventually hired a seminary student to do Christian education, including youth ministry. The seminary student sought my advice on youth ministry. The church was a fairly healthy one, although its youth ministry was in big trouble. Only persons in a certain clique came to the Sunday evening meetings. The others did not come because they knew they weren't wanted. And the ones who did come never did anything constructive. I suggested that the seminary student *cum* youth worker avoid the numbers game, and certainly not embark on an entertainment program. I suggested that she ask the Christian education committee if they would be willing to try another approach to youth ministry. Could they look around to see who was doing what in the church? Who was visiting prisoners? Who was calling on the sick? Who was putting out the newsletter? Who served on the Urban Council? Then the committee could find a young person to be an apprentice to each member of the church who was engaged in mission. Of course the young persons so engaged might rapidly go beyond apprenticeship to a status of being a partner in mission with the adult.

Similarly, the committee could look around to see what the needs are in the church and community, and what talents are possessed by the young persons. Then the young persons could be assigned short-term service projects according to need and talent. The persons involved in service, adults and youth alike, would meet regularly for sharing, support, and prayer. As a final suggestion to the student youth worker, I added, "If no one comes to Sunday evening fellowship, don't worry about it."

The suggested youth program was based on the assumptions that (1) the church exists for mission, (2) young persons are members of the church, and (3) young persons want to do significant things with their lives.

The Message of Discipleship Today

Leaders of youth ministry who seek to take seriously Dietrich Bonhoeffer's message about discipleship, proclaiming it in today's church, could follow five pointers which come from five New Testament words.

Kerygma, or proclamation. Youth ministry must give a clear call. The church must give a direct, straightforward call to young persons to become disciples. The call must be honest and not watered down. It must be sincere, that is, the call must come from a disciple.

Koinonia, or community. Youth ministry must provide strong support from the community of faith. This support comes from peers who hold each other up as they try to be the church together. The support also comes from adult leaders who seek to be disciples along with the young persons. The entire community of faith, the congregation, also is involved in being the base group from which the young persons can practice their discipleship.

Oikumene, or the whole, inhabited earth. Youth ministry must express global aspects of discipleship, beyond the narcissism of self-development. Not only must the youth program help an adolescent see beyond one's self, but it must also go beyond the chauvinism of one's own church. The Christian faith is global and those who practice it can learn much from others. Ultimately there needs to be a solidarity with others as young disciples experience the unity of the church of Jesus Christ and identify with those who have great physical needs but who also have rich spiritual gifts.

Diakonia, or ministry. Youth ministry must involve the real work of ministry. What is asked of the young people is not play acting, or merely preparing for the future, but real deeds of love and service.

Mathētēs, or discipleship. Youth ministry must call for deep commitment. Discipleship means giving up one's life and taking up the cross.

"If [anyone] would come after me, let [that one] . . . take up [the] cross and follow me. For whoever would save [one's] life will lose it; and whoever loses [one's] life for my sake and the gospel's will save it" (Mark 8:35).

2

Attaining the Personhood of Jesus Christ

Adolescence often is known as the period of storm and stress. You probably can recall without much prompting, a number of "stormy weather" experiences from that time of your life. A number of "fair weather" experiences will come to mind as well.

I recall at age sixteen showing off a new used car to my friends. In the course of a U-turn I drove right into a fire hydrant, causing a huge dent in the fender and making an elderly pedestrian almost jump right out of her skin! I also recall that at age fifteen I was asked by the pastor of the church to be the leader and teacher of a junior high club.

As we recall our own adolescence, we can admit that adolescents have a bad press and a poor public image. Depictions of adolescents in movies and on television programs reflect how poorly adults think of adolescents. Among the images are those of rebellion, delinquency, surliness, flightiness, irresponsibility, and so forth. As far as many adults are concerned, teenagers are a trinity of acne, sex, and rudeness. The magazine *National Lampoon* picked up this public image and satirized it in a takeoff on advice columns for teenagers. The column is supposedly written by a noted paragon of social grace and charm, Nancy Reagan!

So You're Growing Up?

Dating is like dynamite. Used wisely, it can move mountains and change the course of mighty rivers. Used foolishly, it can blow your legs off. Scientists have calculated, for example, that if a man could harness even a fraction of the kinetic energy wasted in a single session of Post Office or Spin the Bottle, he could light up the entire city of Wilmington, Delaware, and have enough left over to discover and mass produce a cheap, effective cure for cancer of the larynx. Thus, it is so important to understand and harness the explosive power of the forces developing in your body.

Have you ever noticed that your body is playing little tricks on you lately? If you are a boy, you may have noticed your legs, face, arms and chest are becoming covered with thick, black . . . hairs and your voice may be beginning to sound like a phonograph needle ruining your favorite stack of platters. If you are a girl, you may have noticed a painful swelling up here and some more funny business going on down there.

These dramatic changes can mean only one thing: cholera. If you are not among the lucky ones, then it simply means you are becoming a young man or a young woman, depending on how much fluoride they dumped in your parents' drinking water. I know that such changes can often be difficult for growing teens, but try to weather the storm and "grin and bear it." There is always impotence and menopause.

During these trying teen-age years, a girl begins to "menstruate" (*men* stroo ate), and a boy begins to have "erections" (ee *wreck* shuns), normally only when called to the blackboard by his teacher. There is absolutely nothing abnormal about this, and, aside from voluntary sterilization, no known cure.

Not only is the miracle of growing up taking place inside your body, but it may be going on outside it as well. There are many names for this remarkable stage of development—"acne," "pimples," "blackheads," "whiteheads," "redcaps," "boils," "blemishes," "cankers," "zits," "pustules," "efflorescence," "breaking out," "pockmarks," "carbuncles," "suppurations," "polyps," "goobies," and "St. Anthony's Fire," to mention just a few. Perhaps one of your clever friends will notice this badge of young adulthood and jokingly dub you with an appropriate descriptive nickname, like "Crater Face," "Swiss Cheese," or "Vomithead." But perk up! Such bothersome side effects are all in Mother Nature's master plan, and they may very possibly disappear in time, leaving a healthy, glowing complexion on those portions of your face and neck not permanently disfigured by layers of horny scar tissue.[1]

If adult leaders are to help young persons, a more sympathetic understanding of adolescence is required. Inaccurate and negative stereotypes and myths about adolescence will need to be discarded. Among the myths to be thrown out are five which are identified by Joan Lipsitz, director of the Center for Early Adolescence at the University of North Carolina.[2]

We should discard the myths of adolescence as a period of uniform, synchronized growth, and of homogeneity. These myths claim that every person starts puberty at the same age, goes through bodily changes and growth at the same rate, all in a predictable, uniform pattern. These myths are easy to dispel. In any group, were you to ask ten sixteen-year-old persons to stand, you would find ten different sizes and shapes of persons. They would be in a variety of stages of physical, emotional, social, sexual, and mental development. From your own experience you know that when you were a teenager, you were not like anyone else in the world. While there were similarities with your peers, you would not submit to the charge of being "typical." Your ideas were your own and deserved to be heard as such. Your problems were unique and could not be handled "by the book."

Another myth claims that adolescents are children, or at least they are not yet adults. This myth is not entirely false but is not entirely or helpfully true either. The problem with this myth is its stereotyping which puts individual young persons into confining categories. The story is told by Joan Lipsitz of a fourteen-year-old girl who was sexually active, and who participated in a drug counseling program.[3] In other words, she was already "into a lot of stuff." What "bugged" the girl the most about her parents was that whenever her boyfriend called, the parents would say something such as, "Just a minute, Betsy's outside playing." Maybe some fourteen-year-olds spend their time playing outside, along with other children on the block. But not Betsy. She was no child.

Although persons are reaching puberty as early as age eleven years in North America, and most persons have the physical capability by the time they are thirteen to mate and produce babies, cultural and sociological factors in the society place adolescents in the not-yet-adult category in a way that juvenilizes them and prevents full acceptance of them by adults, who consider themselves mature by comparison.

A similar myth about adolescence states that adolescents and young adults are "going through a stage." They are in transition. This again is true, but not true enough; that is, this truism is an oversimplification which leads to stereotyping. Indeed, adolescents are persons in transition, starting at one point in life development and moving toward another. But it is also true that all persons in every age are in transition. A forty-year-old person is in transition. A seventy-eight-year old person is in transition. All of us are "movin' on."

The problem with this myth is that because adults think of adolescents as persons in transition, they think that what adolescents do does not count or does not matter. "They'll get over it." "Be good, have fun, stay out of trouble, prepare for life, and we'll get back to you when you grow up." The condescension is stifling.

Adolescents know that what they do is real and has personal meaning. Their lives and activities are important. What they do does count and they are not "just foolin' around."

The biggest and most troublesome myth about adolescence is that it is a pathological time in the human life span; that it is a bad time, a sick time, a time in life to pass through, ASAP (As Soon As Possible).

Remember when your mother told you, "I'll be glad when we get through the storm of adolescence"? Or, "You were so cute when you were little—what's happened to you now that you're a teenager?" The message was a veiled hope that you could conveniently disappear for five years and come back as a grown-up.

A large number of teenagers do get in trouble. For some,

the teen years are sick years. But not for all persons, and not for all the time a person is an adolescent. If 2 percent of unmarried teenage girls become pregnant, this also means that 98 percent do not! Such a statistic is no worse than it is for any age group beyond adolescence. To be fair, we must admit that it is not just those between the ages of thirteen and nineteen who are having all the stresses and storms of life. The teen and young adult years may be difficult ones, but then so is every age in life. Every age has its storms and stresses.

The popular notion is that a teen's life can be expected to be stormy; bad weather will be encountered. This expectation, raised to the level of stereotype, may have started with G. Stanley Hall. Hall was the first psychologist to describe the age group of adolescence. In 1904 he wrote *Adolescence: Its Psychology and Its Relation to Physiology, Anthropology, Sociology, Sex, Crime, Religion, and Education.*[4] The phrase, storm and stress, was used in this book and was its emphasis. A bit of self-fulfilling prophecy was at work, for here was an eminent psychologist who told us we would have trouble as adolescents—and we did.

Adolescence as Pilgrimage

To be effective in youth ministry we must get away from the myths and stereotypes of adolescence which emphasize the storms and stresses. Another way to look at adolescence is that it is a time for identity formation.

As so many who work with the young know, the description of adolescence as a time for identity formation comes from the teachings of Erik Erikson. Erikson and his numerous followers see life as a long journey during which a person develops stage by stage, from cradle to grave.[5] Adolescense is one of life's stages on this eventful journey. At this time several factors come together to provide opportunities for persons to deal with the question of identity. The persons are answering the question "Who am I?" By the time a person enters the teen years, much territory has been traversed. Nurturing, training, and educating by parents, schools, society, and peers have taken place. Mental development is at a point where a person can think for one's self. This is an apt time to be putting things together to establish one's own separate, independent identity. The adolescent person can take steps for one's self.

In *The Care and Counseling of Youth in the Church*, Paul B. Irwin summarizes the tasks of adolescent identity formation. He writes of four areas of formation.[6]

1. Finding acceptance within community
2. Deepening interpersonal communication
3. Shaping an ideology or vision of life
4. Achieving vocational direction

Irwin points out that the five to ten years a person spends working on the question "Who am I?" can be likened to a journey or an odyssey. This is a time of great challenges including that of leaving the security of one's home to take a long, uncharted journey. A traveler may have a clear idea of what to look for on the journey but many other travelers have no such clarity. Events happen and surprises spring up. By the time the traveler has returned, she or he has changed and is no longer the same person who started the journey.

Journey is a useful term. But Irwin suggests that the term "pilgrimage," as used by Lewis Sherrill in the classic book on Christian life development *The Struggle of the Soul*,[7] may be even more useful, particularly for Christians. "Journey" conjures the heroic. The stress is upon the development of human virtues while on a heroic journey of exploration and discovery. "Pilgrimage" suggests a search for a certain goal, a holy grail to be given by another, greater One. Pilgrimage suggests the grace of God; a pilgrim is one in search of the gift of the central purpose of life which can result in the gift of faith. If "journey" is useful for its element of human courage and risk, "pilgrimage" is useful for its realization that identity and faith are divine gifts which are given during one's search.

The four tasks of identity formation listed by Paul Irwin can be accomplished by persons during their adolescent pilgrimage in search of self, God, and faith. Two of those tasks have to do with finding acceptance within community and deepening interpersonal communication. These important tasks will be treated in the next chapter. The two other tasks are treated here.

To answer "Who am I?" will require a vision of life. Shaping a vision of life is essential to identity formation. Many young persons know intuitively the need to search for values and goals in life. They know they must have a sense of the transcendent, the power which is beyond one's self. They are capable of thinking thoughts about what is beyond self, and their questions about what constitutes this power drives them toward the transcendent. There is a mystery that is "out there" to be found.

Lest we be too sentimental about the prospects for the discovery of the greater power, or of God, we need to recall the earlier mentions of the conditions in our society which trivialize or deny life. There is today the "psychic toll of the nuclear age"[8] which affects the way we think about life and about the future. Consciously or not, many young persons assume no future. We exist in an age with virtually no sense of hope. The threat of war and nuclear destruction affects all of us as a disease would. There also are other forms of dis-ease which nag at us and cloud our vision. Shaping a vision of life while in the midst of cultural chaos and unremitting pluralism leaves us with the feeling of being too tired and worn out to care what virus it is that has sapped our strength.

Young persons have the task of shaping a vision of life at a time when the world and its inhabitants are not feeling well. An incident reported by church educator Myron Bloy illustrates this situation. Bloy found himself in a circumstance similar to the one recounted in the first chapter of this book. He and his wife were in a meeting of parents and young persons who had gathered at their church to discuss what to do with their youth group. As was characteristic, the youth met in a group separate from their parents. Bloy tells about the parents:

> We parents struggled valiantly with the problem and, when we warmed up to it, came up with a lot of seemingly splendid suggestions: using the parish house as an after-school crafts center where kids could weave, paint, pot, carve, etc. with all the

appropriate tools and skilled resource people at hand; developing a counselling service that would promote group and individual therapy; and creating a community action center that would involve teenagers in tackling some of our local social and environmental problems. We were, in fact, quite pleased with the array of possibilities we had conjured up.[9]

Meanwhile, the young people had spent their time plotting how to change the type of worship practiced in that church, to introduce contemporary elements in worship which they felt would be more spiritual than the old, staid material being said and sung in the church.

Bloy surmised that behind the efforts of the young people was an unarticulated attempt toward a more serious piety. The young people intuitively sensed that the current form of worship in that church was protecting them against the *mysterium tremendum* rather than laying them open to it.[10] The young people wanted to get in touch with God. That was more relevant than making pots or weaving macrame, or even recycling bottles and cans.

We must ask ourselves whether or not we in our churches commit the same sin of omission. In the many fine things we do for young people we may fail to give them a chance to get in touch with God.

Certainly a part of the task of youth ministry is to encourage persons to shape a vision of life, a vision that can see God. What kinds of activities in our churches place young people in the presence of a living, loving God? How can the courses of instruction, retreat and camping experiences, peer-led discussions of contemporary topics, Bible studies, and personal conversations contribute to a young person's ability to articulate a purpose for life and a sense of direction in life? It is a marvel that so many persons do make wise and mature decisions about whom to marry, which issue to become concerned about, what career to pursue, or which group to join. It would be marvelous to be able to say that these persons act out of a vision of life shaped while participating in the youth ministry program of the church.

Related to the shaping of a vision of life is the important

task of achieving vocational direction. On an elementary level this means that the church should help each young person find the best job for himself or herself. Young people need every help they can get to identify their talents and interests and to match these with jobs that are challenging and useful to society. If the youth ministry program does nothing else, it will still have been valuable if it provides a series of meetings to help young people decide on careers. But achieving vocational direction means much, much more. Vocation means calling. God, who gives life and personality to each person, also calls each person. During the young person's identity pilgrimage there is the need to discover what are one's talents, personality, interests, and values. More is needed. These must be understood as gifts from God, and these gifts must be understood as the attributes which enable a person to be a co-creator or co-worker with God in creation. God is a working God who created a working world. Each person is to be a part of this creative working world. To achieve this sense of vocational direction a young person must know one's self and know God. The young person must be a theologian who can see self, world, and work in the light of God's plans and purposes.

Consider the following example of how an adult leader of youth can be a valuable resource for shaping a vision of life and achieving vocational direction. In *The Care and Counseling of Youth in the Church*, Paul Irwin suggests "identity conversations." These are conversations between a youth and an adult on matters of personal decisions, with the possibility that theological dialogue may take place. Young people who are in the decision-making phase of their pilgrimage are invited to talk about it. The decisions may involve choosing a college or a job, or joining the church, or volunteering for summer service. During the conversations, questions such as these can be used:

> As you look ahead to graduation, what do you think you will be doing next year? What tentative ideas do you have about this?
> What are some hopes or thoughts you have as to what you want to be and do, as plans for the future? When did you decide this?

Have you sought information and counsel about it?

If you have time and means some day, what would you most like to accomplish?

How does the world look to you today? Where do things seem to be going? How does this fit with the life you want to live and what you want to do?

Do you see anything in the world and the future that you feel is worth being deeply concerned about, something that people ought to do something about?

Most people get down in the dumps occasionally. Has this happened to you? What was going on?

What three objectives best describe you to yourself?[11]

Not every adult could carry on such a conversation with a young person. Some adults, of course, don't want to. Some are afraid to. But those who are willing will find a sense of fulfillment in raising good questions, hearing what the young person has to say, and in being available to that person. There is a word for the adult who is available to young people in this way: guarantor.

As young people go on pilgrimages of identity and faith formation, they can be supported by guarantors who walk with them. Guarantors can share the burdens of the journey, help read the road signs, and offer encouragement.

A *guarantor* is one who swims across the lake and waves encouragement from the other side. "If I can make it, you can." One who climbs the face of the cliff and holds the rope for the next one coming. A guarantor guarantees. In actions . . . rather than by anything he [or she] says, he [or she] offers support and reassurance: "Life is worthwhile . . . It's O.K. to be you. It's O.K. to have feelings. It's even O.K. to make mistakes."[12]

For the young person a guarantor can be an adult whose actions and personality show the youth what is meant by growing up and by really living. A guarantor can be an advisor and spouse who accept each other, love each other, and show how a man and woman can live and work together. Or a guarantor can be a teacher who shows in his or her own life the importance of intellectual curiosity. Or it could be a grocery clerk who treats teenage customers as human beings, or a coach who is concerned with persons more than with winning.

Young pilgrims need guarantors—role models—who set examples of life. One of the most valuable services adult leaders can render is to serve as guarantors. To a large degree youth ministry leadership involves such service, and when recruiting adults for leadership in youth ministry, the church should keep this in mind. Adults may shrink from such a demanding ministry. But adults and young persons alike can gain strength from a particular guarantor or role model who can help us to be human and to have abundant life. Jesus Christ is the world's guarantor. "For to this you have been called, because Christ also suffered for you, leaving you an example, that you should follow in his steps" (1 Peter 2:21). The Greek word for "example" is *hupogrammos,* the "perfect pattern." In calling Jesus our *hupogrammos,* there is a reference to the primary education of Greek boys, particularly to the way they were taught to write. In those days papyrus was expensive so tablets were used for those who needed to practice writing. These tablets were shadow boxes containing wax. A stylus was used to make the marks, using the pointed end of the stylus for writing and the flat end for smoothing out the wax in order to write on the wax again. The master or teacher would write the words on the tablet which the student copied. The student followed the master's pattern. The master's grooves provided the guidelines. Often the master would take the youngster's hand to guide its strokes. The image in this setting is that learning was not merely a matter of watching some master do an act. What the master did, the student would also do, often with the master doing it along with the pupil. In current terms, learning would involve not merely watching on television as Chris Evert Lloyd hit a tennis ball or listening to the music of Stevie Wonder on a recording. It would be having Lloyd or Wonder do it, then do it with you, to enable you to be able to do it for yourself.

Jesus' own life on earth was a guarantee that our lives can be human and significant too. We learn of life and purpose not merely by the long-distance messages given by God from on high. The Word becomes flesh and dwells among us. God says, through Jesus, "Life can be good. This is how to be human. You can do it. This is how. Jesus is our pattern, our guarantor."

By now you, the reader, may have sensed that we have moved from psychology into theology. Indeed, this has happened, for it is a serious concern for the church that as useful as psychology is for youth ministry, it is not enough. To base youth ministry only on psychological understandings of adolescence, is to ask too much of one discipline. Psychology, sociology, and other disciplines are to be informed by the understandings of theology as well. Identity formation is informed by theology. A young person can see a vision of life by looking at the life of Jesus Christ. We are to ". . . attain to the unity of the faith and of the knowledge of the Son of God, to mature [personhood], to the measure of the stature of the fulness of Christ" (Ephesians 4:13).

In a theological consideration of the adolescent task of identity formation we can learn from what Dietrich Bonhoeffer writes about discipleship and can apply this to identity formation and to youth ministry.

Discipleship and Identity

From Bonhoeffer's book *The Cost of Discipleship*, four concepts are instructive:[13]

1. When Jesus calls us to discipleship, he gives us an identity.
2. When Jesus calls us to discipleship, he gives us his identity.
3. Disciples are peculiar people.
4. Discipleship is a decision for, rather than against, Jesus.

When Jesus calls us to discipleship, he gives us an identity.

The first identification for anyone who follows Jesus Christ is that of *disciple*. This identification should be stressed when we baptize a young person or otherwise have someone join the Christian community. Instead, we think of this person now as a Baptist, or an Episcopalian, or some such designation. Baptisms can be such nice affairs that we forget that baptism symbolizes drowning—dying. Baptism represents the death of the old person and rebirth as a new being. Baptism or any similar act marks a person with a purpose in life. The baptized disciple becomes a minister who joins with Jesus Christ and the other disciples in doing Christ's ministry on earth.

Young persons will find all sorts of ways to form an identity. Those who accept the call to be disciples will find that their identity is defined by their discipleship. (A list of some characteristics of that discipleship will be given later.)

Dietrich Bonhoeffer taught that it is the call to discipleship and our response to it that gives us our individuality. Unlike today's churches which baptize or confirm a whole eighth grade class, Jesus calls each person individually. The only way to respond is alone; no one else can accept a person's discipleship for him or her. The person stands alone, struggles with the decision to respond, and makes an individual choice. Through individual response the person gains an individual identity.

In contemporary terms, a young person's identity, values, and faith are his or her own. They are not those of parents, church, or guarantor. In youth ministry we can model faith or "guarantee" life but the response to discipleship is the individual's to make. Youth ministry programs must allow for that identity-forming individual response.

When Jesus calls us to discipleship, he gives us his identity

In the film *The Antkeeper* a crude but helpful illustration is given. In order to communicate with a colony of ants, to help the ants learn how to do what ants ought to be doing, the human antkeeper's son gives up his status and becomes an ant. In this sacrificial way he shows the way truly to be an ant. The incarnation, the coming of God to us in human form, has a similar effect. We humans find humanness defined and exemplified for us when God gives up godly status and becomes human. However, Jesus is not typically, commonly human but is one who loves others and willingly gives up his life for the sake of others.

Jesus' incarnation affirms humanness and at the same time

calls humans to be loving, self-giving, and sacrificial. Here then is the *hupogrammos* or pattern of life we considered earlier. Bonhoeffer puts it this way:

> Now we can understand why the New Testament always speaks of our becoming "like Christ." We have been transformed into the image of Christ, and are therefore destined to be like him. He is the only "pattern" we must follow. And because he really lives his life in us, we too can "walk even as he walked," and "do as he has done," "love as he has loved," "forgive as he forgave," . . . By being transformed into his image, we are enabled to model our lives on His.[14]

Disciples are peculiar People.

This third point from Bonhoeffer also has application to youth identity formation. Consider how strange, how peculiar, the characteristics seem to our world as they are drawn by Bonhoeffer from the Beatitudes:[15]

1. Jesus' disciples are poor in spirit (they accept privation for Jesus' sake).
2. Jesus' disciples are those who mourn (who mourn the guilt of the world and its fate, and bear sorrow and suffering for the sake of the world).
3. Jesus' disciples are meek (they renounce their own rights and live for the sake of Christ).
4. Jesus' disciples hunger and thirst for righteousness.
5. Jesus' disciples are merciful.
6. Jesus' disciples are peacemakers.
7. Jesus' disciples are persecuted for righteousness' sake.
8. Jesus' disciples are the salt of the earth and the light of the world.

The word "peculiar," as in "peculiar people," is a scriptural term referring to the uniqueness of Christian discipleship. But by today's standards, the "peculiar people" with their Christ-centered way of life would be characterized in modern parlance another way; these people are *weird!*

But that is the identity young people are called by Jesus Christ to accept.

Discipleship is a decision for, rather than against, Jesus Christ.

An observer of modern youth wrote,

> . . . there is a "crisis of commitment" in American society, most apparent among the young. It involves their unwillingness—or inability—to promise anything for the future. Instead, they offer disclaimers: "I don't know how long I'll want to stay with this . . . I want to be free to do my own thing . . . We don't know how we'll feel about each other a year from now." [16]

In contrast to these noncommital ways of life, Bonhoeffer places stark demands of discipleship—a decision must be made for or against Christ. Bonhoeffer was not writing about a series of decisions and a gradual increment of loyalty. He was not writing about deciding whether or not to do this act or that act, or of choosing from a list of options. The question was not similar to asking, "Do you like the way I talk, or the way I fry my eggs?" Rather, the question was: "Are you for me or against me?"

> As they were going along the road, a man said to him, "I will follow you wherever you go." And Jesus said to him, "Foxes have holes, and birds of the air have nests; but the Son of man has nowhere to lay his head." To another he said, "Follow me." But he said, "Lord, let me first go and bury my father." But he said to him, "Leave the dead to bury their own dead; but as for you, go and proclaim the kingdom of God." Another said, "I will follow you, Lord; but let me first say farewell to those at my home." Jesus said to him, "No one who puts his hand to the plow and looks back is fit for the kingdom of God" (Luke 9:57-62).

Who Am I?

The pilgrimage of identity formation is a major task for each young person. We youth workers can use a number of resources as we try to help young persons on this pilgrimage. There are the resources of psychology and sociology and the support of family and church. But Dietrich Bonhoeffer, that radical Christian, pushes us to a radical approach to identity formation. A famous poem by Bonhoeffer, entitled "Who Am I?" offers for us today a summary of the young person's pilgrimage:

Who am I? They often tell me
I stepped from my cell's confinement
calmly, cheerfully, firmly,
like a Squire from his country house.

Who am I? They often tell me
I used to speak to my warders
freely and friendly and clearly,
as though it were mine to command.

Who am I? They also tell me
I bore the days of misfortune
equably, smilingly, proudly,
like one accustomed to win.

Am I then really that which men tell of?
Or am I only what I myself know of myself?
     .....

Who am I? This or the Other?
Am I one person to-day and to-morrow another?
Am I both at once? A hypocrite before others,
and before myself a contemptible woe-begone weakling?
Or is something within me still like a beaten army
fleeing in disorder from victory already achieved?

Who am I? They mock me, these lonely questions of mine.
Whoever I am, Thou knowest, O God, I am thine![17]

3

Becoming the Body
of Christ

For all of us, belonging is a high priority. And so it is for
me. This can be seen from a recounting of some personal
experiences. My life has been lived within the Christian
community and as an ordained minister in the institution of
that community, the church. My professional life has been expressed as a pastor, a program and resource developer on a
denominational agency staff, a seminary professor, and as the
director of the education division of an ecumenical national
church council. Each job has been rewarding and enjoyable.
While I was teaching at the seminary, a decision confronted
me which forced me to examine my priorities in life and work.
I was invited to work for the National Council of the Churches
of Christ in a complex administrative-type job. To do this would
require leaving a small school and close-knit Christian community, strong student-teacher relationships, good faculty
friendships, and a marvelous house in the best part of Texas.
Why would a teacher with tenure and unlimited access to ten-

nis courts want to give up all this for a mess of pottage in New York City?

I experienced much inner struggle. On one occasion I had a long talk with a friend and colleague, a professor of Old Testament. We weighed the pros and cons of staying with the seminary and of joining the council. I do not remember the details, but I do remember one question my friend asked which provoked much thinking and a response from my inner being: "Dave, what do you love the most?"

An automatic response would have been to say that I love most of all, Jesus Christ. This was assumed and did not need to be said. What was wanted was an answer that was specific enough to be helpful in the decision-making process about the invitation to take a new job. So I answered, "I love the church. That's what I love and what has the most meaning for my work. I want what is best for the church. My life is devoted to it."

With this simple answer I recalled a whole lifetime of experiences and commitments. I am a Chinese-American, born and raised in Chinatown, San Francisco. My childhood was basically stable and culturally rich, in a loving although typically reserved family setting where the parents maintain some distance from the children. Growing up in tenement apartments in a crowded urban environment was not easy. Young people in Chinatown lived in the midst of language and cultural clash and knew that their opportunities were limited by racial prejudice and the walled-in horizons of the ghetto. As a young person I observed that most of the people in Chinatown lived with some degree of marginality. They were no longer purely Chinese nor were they fully accepted as Americans; very few persons, it seemed to me, carried a sense of identity which was satisfying to them.

I first knew who I was and gained a sense of belonging when a unique community of faith reached out and called me into it. This community gave me a sense of personal identity and a network of relationships. It offered a purpose and mission in life and provided support. Indeed all that is written in this book about discipleship and community is autobiographical.

I am who I am, I believe what I believe, and I do what I do

because of the way this unique community of faith in Chinatown, San Francisco, called me into it and gave me the gifts of
identity, a vision of life, and belonging. This church was the
force that taught me how to pray, helped me relate my story to
The Story in the Bible, and was the community that heard my
confessions and offered forgiveness and acceptance. It was
through this community that I became involved in mission and
service.

Now I can say, "Belonging is a high priority for me." Participating in a community of faith has molded me into the kind
of person I am, with the values I hold.

What were your experiences of the church as a community
of faith? What has the church taught you about yourself and
your values? How has the church influenced your understanding of the purpose of life and the mission of your life? As leaders of young people, we need to reflect often on such questions.

A Paucity of Models of Community

Were we to give a nickel for every example of a redemptive,
informed, socially active community of faith supporting a similarly active youth ministry, we could pay for this out of our
pocket money and still end up with some change! There are
not many programs of youth ministry which are caring, covenanting, ministering communities of faith. In most churches
youth ministry is a struggle. Attendance is sporadic. The interests of the young people are elsewhere. The activities are
irrelevant in that they neither help the young people to grow
or the church to witness and serve. In some churches the youth
program is highly successful in terms of numbers, activities,
and fun. These churches run high-powered programs which
are planned and conducted by professional youth workers who
can provide good food, good singing, ski trips in the winter
and river trips in the summer, et cetera, et cetera, et cetera.
Yet, after three or four years of either type of youth program,
small and struggling or big and eventful, a young person may
not have heard the good news that God loves her, that she has
an identity and purpose in life, that her sins are forgiven, that
she is called into community, that she has support for her in-

dividuality and a place for corporate action and witness. Whole generations of young people will pass through our youth programs and never hear the Gospel.

While interviewing a job applicant recently, I learned that this highly talented person had decided not to move his family from New York to Chicago when his organization moved. His two teenage sons were involved in a good church with a solid youth ministry program. He was willing to take a lesser job so that the two boys could stay with that church and youth group. I admired this person's perceptions and values and envied him. Our family had no such luck; during their ten years of adolescence our two boys did not find and never participated in a church that could be considered to have a good youth program. We have two "ecclesiastically deprived" young men in our family.

Belonging to a supportive community is a basic human need. Like people in any age group, young people want and need to belong to a group that understands and accepts them. In early years the family provides this sense of belonging. But during adolescence there is a natural need to look beyond the family and to move toward independence. So the peer group becomes very important and for most young people the peer group is the place of belonging. Not every peer group, however, offers positive identity formation, high moral values, concern for others, or concern for faith. In search for a place of belonging, a "meaningful space," some young people join an exotic group— a cult group perhaps—which offers a sense of belonging and meaning. Sometimes the search for belonging leads young persons into the mass gatherings of rock concerts, pep rallies, and the like. Yet, according to a youth worker quoted in *Young People and Their Culture,* much of today's peer culture leaves youth with "a sense of grayness, emptiness, meaninglessness, confusion, despair."[1] It's the pits.

Peer culture, along with some other forms of community, serves to reinforce certain societal standards such as individualism and competition. Such forms of community do not operate as places to challenge people to a better life. A perceptive youth minister and teacher, Bill Myers, points out that peer culture can be like a pyramid.[2] Especially in suburban schools, Myers sees young people competing against each other, climbing over each other to reach the top. What Myers tried to do in his church was to provide another model: not a pyramid but a circle.

The church is a circle. It is a time and a place for people to process their histories, values, beliefs, and actions in a caring community.

Before describing how this circle, the church, works, let us look at one more problem which exemplifies the paucity of models of community. We in the church may be restricting our ability to help young persons, particularly our ability to provide communal experiences for them, because of the narrow way in which we understand young people. Much research has been done on adolescent development. Church educators have benefited greatly from that research. But a major portion of the research has been psychological in nature, and a major portion of what educators have appropriated from research has also been psychological in nature. We have tended to think of each young person in terms of individual growth, such as individual cognitive development, individual sexual development and identity, and individual decisions and behaviors. Therefore, we have tended to design programs to help an individual to grow. But in doing so, we have developed a huge blind spot by neglecting the social aspects of the life of the adolescent.

Gwen Kennedy Neville, a professor of sociology who wrote several revealing books on church groups and the influence of social customs and culture on these groups and their members, urges youth ministry leaders to develop their "ethnographic skills."[3] This does not mean skills in working with ethnic groups, as noble as that may be. Ethnographic skills are those that enable a leader to see what is happening with individuals in their various natural social settings. A youth leader who observes young people in their groupings, and notes their gatherings and dispersals, arrangement of space, use of time, and organization of social units, is using ethnographic skills. Listening to the language and words, and the symbols, would provide the observer with clues to the values and beliefs of the group and its members. Being able to come up with a social description of young people gives the adult leader a fuller picture of the experiences and the world of youth.

Given our intention to invite young people into the body of Christ, we can enhance our potential by using ethnographic skills. Three benefits are possible: reality, holism, and communal ministry.

Being able to learn about the social settings of young people enhances the possibility of reality for youth ministry. For better or for worse, Christians, particularly "professional Christians" such as ministers, often are insulated from the realities of common life. Because of our age, interests, and responsibilities, we adult leaders do not spend much time in arcades, school cafeterias, fast food emporia, shopping malls, school rallies and games, teen parties, and dances. On Saturday nights we may be busy preparing a lesson or sermon and are not likely to be driving up and down a main street. Consequently we miss much of the energy, dynamics, and mores which inform and influence adolescent behavior. Our study and discussion topics may be on target (everyone is interested in life, identity, acceptance, making choices, and so forth) but we often fail to connect with young persons because we are unable to understand their perspectives, language, symbols, and social influences. The valuable concerns and messages of the church are not communicated to young people because they are not realistic to the experience of youth. To relate with young people we need to know their world. This is not to say that we must become like teenagers; that is a silly notion. It is to say that we will have more realistic and relevant programs for young persons when we know their social settings.

The application of ethnographic skills to youth ministry engenders holism. The ministry is formed to deal with whole persons in whole settings rather than with disembodied mental images in individual settings. It should be self-evident that no young person exists alone but is intricately involved in family, peer, school, and community groups. Nevertheless, adult leaders often forget this or are too lazy to deal with it. Instead, we try to relate to the young person with virtually no reference to the people and social pressures which deeply affect that individual. For example, with no regard for that person's family, work, social situation, or financial resources, we might ask a young person to come to a weekend retreat.

A more holistic approach also views the individual as a whole person and is not satisfied merely to reach the person's intellect with Sunday church school teachings, or merely to play on the person's emotions in a program based on enthusiasm and sentiment. Some suggestions for a comprehensive and balanced youth ministry program will be offered later in this chapter.

A third benefit derived from ethnographic skills is the desire to provide a communal ministry. When it is seen that no adolescent is an island unto herself or himself, it may also be seen that the youth program needs to be a group program. Individual growth takes place in the context of social relationships. Much of the programming uses the dynamics of group processes to give each person in the group the creative, healing, and challenging interaction of others in the group. The group itself is a factor affecting the individual. Two individuals in the youth group may choose not to go off on their own during an outing because they have committed themselves to be a part of the group and to participate in the group's common activity. Such decisions and their social implications, multiplied by the thousands, provide a communal environment and give insight to the young persons concerning what it means to be a member of the body of Christ. A communal youth ministry is an enactment of the community of faith.

Community and Ministry

As we strive to rediscover or reinvent youth ministry, we can look once again at the writings of Dietrich Bonhoeffer. Four ideas about the nature of the Christian community, set forth in Bonhoeffer's little book *Life Together*,[4] provide us with theological guidelines for our youth ministry:

1. Community is a creation of Jesus Christ, not a human creation.
2. Community is a gift.
3. Community is the setting for ministry with one another.
4. Community is the setting for confession and communion.

Community is a creation of Jesus Christ, not a human creation.

Lest we become sentimental about the nature of the youth ministry community, we can be reminded by Bonhoeffer's insight that community is not a human creation. Today we could say it this way: Youth ministry is not all fun and games. The leaders who perceive youth ministry primarily as fun and games, fortunately, are few in number and the hope is that their number will decrease! Nevertheless, a large number of leaders concern themselves with the task of building up the youth group, using a variety of interesting and stimulating group processes so that the participants can "get in touch with each other." Community building becomes the foremost if not sole activity for the group, a thing unto itself. Actually, community building among young persons is not all that hard to do. Given the common tendency of adolescents to seek peer acceptance and support, an enthusiastic and earnest leader can use recreational activities and evoke expressions of good spirit so that the young people soon are shouting and singing, "Our youth group is the best in town." A favorite strategy used by some independent Christian youth organizations is first to secure the appearance of the most attractive youth and then to use their presence to attract other young persons. This may explain why so many quarterbacks and pep team captains become "Christian."

Most groups avoid the crassness of manipulating people and methods in order to draw large numbers of people and to create group spirit. But even such groups that do ought to pay heed to Bonhoeffer's point about the source of community. A church or its youth group is not Christian or communal simply because it has done well in creating such a community. True community, according to Bonhoeffer, is not manufactured by human effort; it is created in and through Jesus Christ. Jesus Christ forgives and accepts you. He calls you into his community. Jesus Christ forgives and accepts me. He calls me into his community. That we are in the same community is because of the work of Jesus Christ. It is through the power of Christ that each of us individuals has been able to set aside our self-consciousness and self-centeredness, to enter into and be committed to a community beyond ourselves. If we have any community—any acceptance of each other—it is because we have one thing in common: Jesus Christ.

In the youth ministry community we are not together because we come from the same high school or because we hold the same cultural heritage and values. Nor are we together because we are of the same age or because we like one another. We are together because Jesus Christ has called us together— that is our only basis for community.

Given the very obvious need for young people to feel comfortable with each other and to gain support for the tasks of identity formation and the forming of relationships, it may seem illogical to us to denigrate our efforts at community building. However, Bonhoeffer's point, harsh as it is, is necessary. If we are to be disciples, we cannot afford to allow personal, human priorities to slip between us and the One who is sovereign over us. The community that we leaders create, however sincere and well-intended, runs the risk of being a humanly manufactured community which serves human interests and needs. Such a community may find itself making choices to keep the group going at all costs, or to do that which is good for the group. It will choose to honor and maintain itself rather than follow Christ.

The community created by Jesus Christ is radically different. It harbors no illusions about the group being good because of how good the people in it are or how well they have done. It is entirely beside the point to think in terms of being the best youth group in town, or the one in which the members get along with each other best, or the one with the most attractive activities. The point is to be a youth group that relies on the saving grace of Jesus Christ for its existence and which strives to be faithful to Christ.

Community is a gift.

Following the radical logic of Bonhoeffer, we can see that if community is not our own creation but that of Jesus Christ, then the community we do experience is a gift. We may have learned this truth from experience first of all and then articulated it as a theological point after some reflection on the experience. Perhaps your youth group became aware of a particular need in your neighborhood. Some commitments were made and through study, the hammering out of plans, and much struggling with the problems, action was taken by the youth group. There probably was no overt effort toward community building; yet when the entire project was over, everyone in the group felt closer to one another than before. The people in the group discovered, as a bonus or gift, a sense of community.

By focusing on the task—the mission—the participants in the project were able to give of themselves and to "get beyond themselves." While there was no guarantee that community would emerge, the participants discovered that their mutual efforts, however successful they were, were also occasions for becoming better acquainted, relating more closely, and accepting and trusting each other more fully. Community was the gift.

The theological perspectives on community which are described in Bonhoeffer's *Life Together* reflect his own experiences of community. Bonhoeffer lived with about thirty seminary students in Finkenwald in an underground situation for about two years during the Nazi regime in Germany. It was not safe to be a part of that group. But focusing on their mission rather than on their own safety or comfort, these fledgling ministers studied, worshiped, and worked together under cover. They wanted to become ministers and one result was that they also became a community. Community was a gift of grace. They discovered in the midst of danger and pressure much comfort, support, and joy in their life together.

We may never be called to as dramatic a situation as were the German theological students studying with Bonhoeffer. Even so, to be a youth ministry group in North America today requires a similar dedication to mission. A youth group must resist being squeezed into a conforming mold by worldly standards. In its exercise of discipleship, the group must be as willing to follow the promptings of the Spirit of Christ as was Bonhoeffer's group, and as open as they were to whatever results and benefits might be given by God.

In another section we will explore the possibility that youth programs ought to engage heavily in social and recreational activities. For now the emphasis is on our commitment to Christ, which places our priorities on being faithful disciples. Disciples expect demanding and lonely missions, and gratefully receive any support or experience of community as a precious gift.

In effect, we are saying to the young persons we invite into the youth ministry, "Come and join us in our mission. It will be hard work. We have no certainty of any reward, except for the reward of knowing Jesus Christ and becoming a part of his company of disciples."

Community is the setting for ministry with each other.

The underground seminary at Finkenwald was more than a school for the thirty or so persons learning the Bible and theology from each other. That underground school was also the setting for some other meaningful activities including worshiping together, studying the Bible in small groups, listening, forgiving, accepting, and tending to each other's needs. The organization and activities of the group were the means by which the members ministered to each other. If we can jump from a comparison of the Finkenwald setting to that of a youth ministry program, we can imagine that ministry can take place in our groups too. Through studying, praying, and singing together, and, yes, through playing together as well as working jointly, it is possible for adults and youth to minister to one another.

The members of the youth group, youth and adults alike, have needs for worship, for the Word which comes from small group Bible study, and for the forgiveness and acceptance which is mediated through the group. Activities and programs are of major significance in youth ministry because they are the means by which persons share faith with one another and work together in fulfillment of their discipleship. Some of this happens during traditional activities such as church school, prayer group, or Bible study. It is not hard to imagine much of this ministry taking place during a weekend retreat. Ministry also occurs during the excitement of a volleyball game, yard work at the church, and a heated debate in youth council. For example, it could be during a debate in youth council that members of the group take a stand for justice and loving concern for the oppressed, possibly victims of peer group oppression in their own school community. There could be a wrestling with the moral teachings of Jesus, and relevant application of these ideals to real situations. Such a debate could be good teaching and learning, in which young people think through an issue theologically and move toward faithful action. Ministry has taken place.

What a difference it would make to an adult leader of youth to be able to understand all youth activities as opportunities for ministry! Then the possibilities for teaching, enabling, supporting, and sharing are endless. Inexperienced or shortsighted adult leaders may believe that young people can be helped only in certain prescribed settings, such as during the final minutes of a Sunday church school hour. In contrast, adult leaders who hold the premise that youth ministry is the setting for ministry with each other will perceive all kinds of opportunities in all kinds of activities for acts of ministry. Such leaders will find no activity too mundane for ministry. Instead, they constantly give thanks to God for all the occasions for sharing, giving, leading, teaching, facilitating, and witnessing. The youth community is the setting for ministry with each other.

Community is the setting for confession and communion.

The complaint was made earlier in this chapter that young people today live in a society constructed more like a pyramid than a circle. Life is understood as a place for aggressive competition and the accumulation of material and social benefits for one's self and family. Not many constructive models of communal living are available. Where can a person feel free to be one's self and to have a secure sense of belonging? If anywhere, it would be the church. *Wrong!* Dietrich Bonhoeffer found the church to be where people had to lie and cheat to stay in it. They had to pretend to be good. One reason why so many young people leave the church or remain cynical about it is that they see this pretense. In *Life Together* Bonhoeffer puts the problem this way:

> The pious fellowship permits no one to be a sinner. So everybody must conceal his sin from himself and from the fellowship. We dare not be sinners. Many Christians are unthinkably horrified when a real sinner is suddenly discovered among the righteous. So we remain with our sin, living in lies and hypocrisy. The fact is that we *are* sinners![5]

A breakthrough occurs when someone in the community admits to being a sinner and does so to another person in the community. This is a breakthrough to the cross, to certainty, and to community. Confessing our human faults to someone else and hearing from that person that Jesus Christ loves and forgives us makes forgiveness and acceptance a reality. There is no need for the sinner to hide. The sinner is allowed to be one's self, which is to be human. The reconciliation which is offered to the sinner who confesses is concrete. It is communicated by a flesh and blood sister or brother in Christ and not in some abstract form. There is real confession and there is real forgiveness, not just idealized, abstract wishes.

It is not likely that you will run out to set up little confession booths in the youth fellowship room. However, you must take seriously the possibility that the youth ministry community is the setting in which young persons can deal with their humanity and can honestly face up to the reality of their failure and sin, and need for redemption. In the youth ministry community a young person can be heard. He or she can hear the good news that "you are accepted." Young people will find that they are in a circle, not a pyramid.

Implications for Youth Ministry

Several broad implications for youth ministry can be found

in Bonhoeffer's thoughts about community. Youth ministry should be relational, holistic, and Christian.

In earlier chapters it has been brought out that during the pilgrimage of identity formation, a young person needs to find acceptance within community and to deepen interpersonal communication. These are relational needs to be addressed through youth ministry. Implicit is the need to balance the common, popular educational activities with other activities. There should be events in which the emphasis is on relating with people and not just on learning information. Those activities which are primarily educational, such as Sunday church school, should allow for ways of learning that are relational. Much of the essence of the Christian faith is relational and can be learned best by using social methods. A young Christian gains a richer appreciation for the nature and authority of the Bible when he or she learns how to read and interpret it in a small group and in corporate worship. The Christian faith is much more than an individual's intellectual assent to a set of doctrines. The faith has communal aspects which are impressed upon a believer by participation in meaningful relationships. Just as it would be ludicrous for a teacher to say to a class, "I'm going to teach you the love of God even if I have to beat it into you!", it is inconsistent with the Christian faith to say, "You can learn how to be a Christian all by yourself."

It is beyond the scope of this book to deal with the endemic individualism and personal piety which is the popular expression of Christianity in North America. What can be said is that a place where this problem can be faced is in the church's youth ministry where the faith which is practiced and taught is corporate and relational.

To provide for the needs of persons in their wholeness, the church's program must be comprehensive, well-rounded, and balanced. As stated earlier, youth ministry should be holistic. This is not a new idea but it does need reiteration. The church in San Francisco which had a large youth ministry program has been guided by the statement of holism in Luke 2:52— "Jesus increased in wisdom and in stature, and in favor with God and [people]." This verse became the outline for a program including activities to enhance mental, physical, spiritual, and social growth. A large mural in the church's community center bears the inscription "Prayer, study, work, and worship."

A very similar outline for church programming is found in one of the most important books on Christian education in the last twenty-five years, *Where Faith Begins*,[6] by C. Ellis Nelson. Nelson, taking his cue from the biblical story of God's relationship with God's people, advocates an educational program that is filled with events. It is in events that educational ministry takes place. The events can be planned in four areas: worship—which incubates faith; fellowship—which makes faith operational; searching (study)—which gives faith meaning; and confronting issues—which makes faith ethical.

Maria Harris, who brings a Roman Catholic sacramental background to her understanding of the church's educational ministry, makes the same point about holism by using the original Greek New Testament terms to outline the ministries to be performed with young persons: *didache*—the ministry of teaching; *leiturgia*—the ministry of prayer; *koinonia*—the ministry of communion; *kerygma*—the ministry of advocacy; and *diakonia*—the ministry of troublemaking, that is, of prophetic social witness.[7]

One more outline for a holistic youth ministry can be mentioned. In this case the outline is pictorial and symbolic, in the form of the mark from a branding iron. This logo comes from Harrison Taylor, program director at Mo-Ranch, a conference center in Texas. Within the wagon wheel design can be discerned four alphabet letters, two of which are drawn in regular fashion and two in reverse: D for *diakonia,* and D in reverse for *didache* (teaching); and K for *koinonia,* and K in reverse for *kerygma*.

A final implication to draw from Bonhoeffer's thoughts about community is this: Youth ministry should be Christian. As described by Bonhoeffer, community is Christ-centered. It is not based on human intentions or achievements. In like manner, youth ministry, as a form of the community of Christ, must be Christian, or Christ-centered. The church's concern for the

personal and spiritual formation of its youth, and for their incorporation into the church, is in response to Christ's command to love and serve these young persons. The church proclaims Christ's call to these persons to join his community of disciples.

This Christian focus is stated clearly in "The Objective of Christian Education for Senior High Young People," written by an interdenominational committee of the National Council of the Churches of Christ:

> The objective of Christian education is to help persons to be aware of God's self-disclosure and seeking love in Jesus Christ and to respond in faith and love—to the end that they may know who they are and what their human situation means, grow as sons [and daughters] of God rooted in the Christian community, live in the Spirit of God in every relationship, fulfill their common discipleship in the world, and abide in Christian hope.[8]

4

Leading by Serving

Lionel Guitar is a young seminarian. He plays the guitar very well. He is athletic, outgoing, attractive, and makes friends easily. Lionel dropped out of the church when his family moved around a lot, but recently had certain experiences that led him to enter seminary. He hopes to get a better picture of the church through his seminary courses.

Mary Cook Baker is a middle-aged mother of two teens. She is regular in church attendance but has no training or skills in working with youth.

Grandpa Moses is hovering around sixty-eight years of age, maybe more. He is in good health and is a longtime member of the church. He knows the Bible and Christian beliefs fairly well and has served the church in various capacities, but is better known for his quietness than his public appearances. He prefers to listen rather than talk.

Youth Leaders Are Ordinary People

If you were recruiting leaders for the youth ministry in your church, which of the three persons would you choose?

If the church could do so, it might be smart to choose all three to serve as a team. There is a decided advantage to having a variety of adults serving as guarantors, presenting different approaches to the faith. But if you could choose but one, consider Grandpa Moses. You need to be wary that Lionel Guitar would try to do youth ministry on the basis of his sparkling personality. He might show much glitter but little substance. Mary Cook Baker may be willing to take her turn because her two children are in the youth program. That in itself may be a good reason to wait a few years before asking her; there is no one more skittish than the parent of an adolescent. Grandpa Moses won't be able to play soccer with the youth group. But then it is not likely that he would try to be a kid. It is quite acceptable that he is quiet; that may become his greatest strength as an adult leader of youth.

Next to the young persons themselves, adult leaders are the most important component of youth ministry. They are more important than curriculum, facilities, and programs. There cannot be a strong youth ministry unless there are strong leaders. However, the title of this chapter is "Leading by Serving." Adult leaders need to have the strength and authority of a servant.

Reflect for a few minutes on how you became a leader of youth.

Perhaps the following profile of a youth leader matches what you and your colleagues in youth ministry showed when you were recruited:

1. A youth leader is good-natured.
2. A youth leader is sociable.
3. A youth leader is helpful.
4. A youth leader is loyal.
5. A youth leader is available.

The first four attributes don't matter so long as you are available!

The probable sequence of experiences which occurred when you were recruited is this:

1. You were drafted, perhaps walking into a bit of a trap.
2. You were given little or no pre-service training.
3. You learned youth ministry by doing it, by trial and error.
4. Because you did not drop out, eventually your faithfulness was rewarded with more work and some training given in a regional workshop.
5. You have risen to a position of recruiting and training others for youth ministry leadership.

The last time I served as a youth ministry leader was in Austin. When our own children got out of junior high school, I was willing to serve on the junior high youth fellowship leadership team. Of the many experiences of that term of service, several come to mind.

My first experience of youth ministry during that time came in August, prior to any youth fellowship meetings in the new program year. Four of us adult leaders got together to get acquainted and to plan the Sunday evening programs for the junior highs. (There were no junior highs present because there had been no carryover from the previous year.) In addition to me, there were a young married couple recently graduated from college and a middle-aged woman, who was the team captain. We agreed to try for a regular pattern of meetings. The first Sunday of the month would be for discussing a topic of interest to the junior highs, using a guide such as *Explore*[1] and similar resources which enabled junior highs to share in peer leadership. On the second Sunday the group would attend the monthly churchwide supper and program. The third Sunday would be for a social, recreational program. The fourth Sunday would be for a service project, study of the church in mission, or a field trip to visit a social service program. We felt good about our first leaders' meeting because we were able to establish a pattern of youth fellowship meetings which had variety and balance.

One Sunday evening for our peer discussion program a dozen of us piled into the leaders' cars and we went to see *The China Syndrome*, a film about a nuclear plant disaster. Afterwards we drank hot chocolate in the little cottage of the young couple on our leadership team. (The junior highs were favorably impressed with the simple furnishings.) Through a series of questions the young people talked about the crisis presented in the movie and identified which characters in the story tried to act with moral conviction. We speculated that if Christ were at work through people in the story, which persons might he have been working through? Which were "crucifixion situations" and which were "resurrection situations?"

Another time the junior high fellowship went camping at a nearby state park. It rained most of that weekend but we managed to have a good time. The young people cooperated beautifully. At the end, sixteen of us crowded around two picnic tables and we asked the junior highs to offer thanks for whatever they wanted to be thankful for. Then we ate lunch and went home.

One Sunday evening only one junior high girl showed up. The four adult leaders and one junior high person played Frisbee for thirty or forty minutes. It seemed like an eternity, especially in the early minutes when we kept glancing at the gate to see who also might show up. But we were talking all that time, about school, about brothers, about a father who worked a thousand miles away in a Colorado oil field, about friends and lack of friends.

The attendance of the Sunday evening group fluctuated between one and fifteen in number. Usually there were six to eight participants. Some programs turned out very well, others were so-so, and some were downright duds. At the end of the year the team leader and her family moved, I had to drop out because of time pressures, and the young couple stayed on as team leaders for the next year.

As far as I'm concerned, for youth ministry in that church it was a very good year.

What was good about it? The church got a team of adults to commit themselves to the young persons. There was a balance of activities, including mission and service programs. Every young person who wanted it, got some attention from an adult. The leaders were willing to share with the young persons that they were followers of Jesus Christ. We all participated in the congregation's activities.

Not all adult leaders end up with such good feelings about their involvement in youth ministry. Often adults are pressed into service without adequate preparation or a clear sense of goals. Usually it is not the fault of the leaders. Sometimes a church has no goals, or has inadequate goals. It is disheartening that for so many churches the reason they have youth ministry is that they've always had youth ministry.

Another reason why some adults feel bad about their involvement is because they are weak in methodology. A part of the problem is that these adults have not had training and do not know which methods are appropriate for the age group. The leaders do not know how to ask a question or to plan and lead a game, or to involve young persons in planning. The adults often end up teaching as they were taught and leading as they were led. Almost always this means using methods which are twenty years out of date.

Another part of the problem is that many adult leaders unwittingly use incongruent methods, such as that mentioned earlier, when a leader says, "I'm going to teach you the love of God even if I have to beat it into you!" A more common incongruency occurs when a church and its youth ministry apply individualistic and moralistic methods. The young people are urged to say a prayer, lead a discussion, or show up for a work project because "it's good for you." Sometimes what is communicated is, "Do this and we will think well of you" or "This is what you must do to please God." Individualism, competition, and moralism are contradictions of the gospel. When leaders behave in these ways or urge the young persons so to behave, our actions speak louder than our words.

A third reason for feeling bad about our youth ministry leadership experiences is that it often seems that we are conducting leadership by crisis. The initial crisis is the lack of leadership itself. The church scraped the bottom of the barrel, it seems, to recruit us in the first place. Leading the youth group seems to be one crisis after another or, in theological terms, "one damned thing after another." We encounter discipline problems. The young persons we counted on fail to show up. The deacons step in to forbid something. The fuses blow. Guest speakers get their dates mixed up. One thing after another happens in crisis fashion. The crisis style of youth ministry is episodic. There is no continuity, no sense of direction, or movement toward a goal. What occurs in one event has no connection with the next.

Finally, a problem adult leaders have regarding methodology is uncertainty about how to apply the words of the Bible and the concepts of Christian theology to the lives of the young people and to the program of youth ministry. If there are applications, they are not easily evident to the leaders. This may be the greatest frustration, not to know how biblical and theological resources relate to youth ministry.

In frustration a church turns to an easy answer, a quick fix. Hire a seminary student! Find a young leader with some charisma! One cannot help but think of a Western movie in which the townspeople are frustrated by their inability to cope with the town bully. They send for a gunfighter—a hired gun. Churches send for a hired guitar.

We adult leaders are ordinary mortals called to do a very difficult task. Is there any help?

Youth Leaders Are Charismatic

Charisma has gotten a bad name. Adult leaders of youth really ought to be charismatic, in the sense of being persons who receive the gift of the Holy Spirit. The snide remarks about guitar-playing, winsome leaders may simply show that the author is jealous of their talent and good looks (and good luck). All leaders of youth must take seriously the gifts that are theirs, given to be used. God is not abstract and usually does not work through abstractions but through real people. These may be wonderfully talented or may be ordinary people. Whatever the case, these people are like chosen vessels, carrying God's treasure, or like ambassadors, God making God's appeal through them.

Faithful women and men have allowed the Holy Spirit of God to work through them. They have lived their lives and "done their thing," not for self-advantage or vain glory but for the glory of God. These people have become leaders and used their personalities and talents unabashedly to convey to young people in a personal way the power of the gospel. You may have seen such a leader in action or exercised such leadership yourself: the right smile at the right time, the graceful gesture, the athletic movement, the artistic result. It seems like magic. The young persons soon learn it is not magic, because you told them so. You helped them to recognize and acknowledge the power of the Holy Spirit. What a charismatic leader does is done in the name of Jesus Christ and for his sake. Humility emerges even from the most brilliant of leadership acts. The leader is able to communicate that what was accomplished was by the power of the Spirit.

When I was a young person, my pastor was that way. He was a brilliant person, a genius at doing youth ministry. He knew how to organize for youth ministry, what to teach, and how to teach it. He knew which book of the Bible the church needed to wrestle with at the right time. He was a great camper and storyteller, a fun song leader, and he presented very moving devotional services. He was much, much more than this. But the true measure of this leader was that those who came under his influence were somehow led to God. Of the hundreds of young persons influenced by this pastor, I do not recall any who claimed that he was their hero. They all saw through him—to Jesus Christ. Through this charismatic leader the young persons saw Jesus Christ.

In youth ministry there are some look-alikes, those who look as if they have charismatic leadership. But there is a way to tell them apart. The look-alikes are not disciples. They love themselves more than they love Jesus Christ. The only disciples they win are not for Jesus Christ but for themselves. They use their personalities and talents to get the young people to follow them rather than to follow Jesus.

Youth Leaders Are Servants

Youth leaders may be ordinary people, and they can be charismatic. They are also servants. They lead by serving.

A genuinely charismatic leader receives the gift of the Holy Spirit. In turn, this leader seeks to make a gift of herself or himself to the young people. The leader seeks to become their servant, a "servant leader" who ministers to the people. Once again we can turn to the wise and radical thoughts of Dietrich Bonhoeffer for guidance. In a simply written yet profound chapter on ministry in the book *Life Together*,[2] Bonhoeffer describes five acts of ministry that members of a community can perform for one another:

1. The ministry of listening.
2. The ministry of helpfulness.
3. The ministry of bearing.
4. The ministry of proclaiming.
5. The ministry of authority.

A brief look at these ministries will provide some basic ideas on how to do youth ministry.

In describing *the ministry of listening,* Bonhoeffer explains that while many people are seeking an ear that will listen, they do not find it among Christians because Christians are too busy talking! Is a youth ministry leader's time so valuable that he or she must use it for talking? Is there no time for listening? Only the person who is committed to the young people will take the time to listen to them. For one thing, it cannot be predicted when a young person will want to talk. More often than not, someone who wants and needs to talk must do it "right now," which is when the leader is busy. Or "right now" may be eleven o'clock at night, which is not the leader's best time. Very often a young person will not get around to the real subject until a lengthy time of probing has elapsed, during which the young person tests to see if the adult can be trusted. The leader who is a willing listener is one who has signalled that she or he is available. Deeper than that, this leader has signalled that she or he cares about the young people.

The true listener listens with more than half an ear. Bonhoeffer reminds us that the listener does not presume to know what the talker has to say. The listener must resist the thought,

"I've heard this before." A more creative thought would be, "This is Barbara (or Joe, or Jennie) and I need to hear what Barbara has in mind." The adult leader who truly respects the young person who is talking will let that person have his or her say.

The second ministry is that of *active helpfulness*. The examples of helpfulness given by Bonhoeffer in *Life Together* are of little things, small acts done in practical ways. These deeds take time and often seem like interruptions. It may be the deed of helping a young person set up chairs for worship, or helping with a rehearsal, or going to the store with a young person to pick up some snacks for a meeting. Such acts of helpfulness are seldom of large consequence. The adult leader leads by serving. By doing so, the leader once again demonstrates trustworthiness and shows respect for the young person.

The theme of ministering to others continues in the third act of ministry, that of *bearing*.

> It is . . . the *freedom* of the other person . . . that is a burden to the Christian. The other's freedom collides with [one's] own autonomy, yet [one] must recognize it. [The Christian] could get rid of this burden by refusing the other person [that person's] freedom. . . . The freedom of the other person includes all that we mean by a person's nature, individuality, endowment. It also includes [that person's] weaknesses and oddities, which are such a trial to our patience, everything that produces frictions, conflicts, and collisions among us. To bear the burden of the other person means involvement with the created reality of the other, to accept and affirm it, and, in bearing with it, to break through to the point where we take joy in it.[3]

We bear the young person to the point where that person realizes we consider him or her to be a free and independent human being, worthy of our love and respect. This form of bearing is one way we affirm a young person's individual identity. We say, in effect, "You are who you are and I will let you be that. I respect you."

Ministry with young persons starts with the genuine respect shown to the young persons by the adult.

We may use the *ministry of proclaiming* less often than other forms of ministry. Preaching too much may lessen the impact of the words we use. But Bonhoeffer emphasizes that there will be times when we must speak up and speak out. If our brother or sister needs correction, we may need to speak a word of correction. This word will not be given as from an all-wise adult to an uninformed youth, but as from a forgiven sinner to another sinner, to share the experience of forgiveness and grace. In the course of youth ministry activities, many "teachable moments" will arise when we can proclaim a word of good news. Especially if the leader has gained the trust of the young people by being faithful to them in many, many ways, and by working with them in numerous projects, the word of proclamation may be listened to.

Bonhoeffer was right on target when he wrote that too many times the golden opportunity to proclaim the word of grace comes but we remain silent or talk about some trivia.[4] It need not be that way. One time I was substitute-teaching a ninth grade church school class. Frankly, I was "winging it," trying to teach without adequate preparation. In reaction to a point I tried to make, one of the students asked, "OK, OK, but what do *you* think? What do you believe?" Every memory of my Rogerian training in counseling said to me not to answer her question but to help the students to answer it for themselves. Everything I had ever written about discovery learning told me that personal belief is something the participants must discover for themselves. But something made me give a twenty-minute statement in which I told those ninth grade persons how, through the life and ministry of Jesus Christ, I had come to believe in God. I told my story.

The girl who had asked the question thanked me for my answer and said it was the first time in her nine years of attending church school that an adult was willing to tell her that he believed, and what he believed.

"Whoever would be great among you must be your servant" (Mark 10:43). In explaining the *ministry of authority*, Bonhoeffer quotes this saying of Jesus.[5] The message can be applied to youth ministry. The adult leader with the best chance of gaining the respect of the young people is not the dominating look-alike of a charismatic leader or necessarily the one with the most impressive biblical knowledge. The respected leader is the one who leads by ministering and serving.

It is the disciple, the servant-follower, who can most authoritatively lead a young person to the servant Lord, the one whose own authority is that of the cross. This understanding of leadership goes against virtually everything the young person sees in the world. Particularly in the North American world, the point is to be "Number One." The concern that the world exhibits is for the self. The goal is to win and not to lose. Jesus Christ authorizes us as leaders to exemplify just the opposite. We are not to be master or mistress, but servant. We are to give up our lives. We are leaders in youth ministry not for ourselves but for the sake of the young persons and of the gospel.

Youth Leaders Share the Koinonia

The most important point of all for understanding youth leadership as ministry is that adult leaders share with the young persons the *koinonia* or community of Christ. The major function of the leader is to help young persons to experience the corporate nature of the Christian faith. The church is the community of acceptance, ministry, and corporate action. To be a disciple is to be a part of the Christian community. But no adult can help a young person enter into a caring, covenanting community unless he or she is a part of a caring, covenanting community, too. What you do not have, you can hardly share.

Most, if not all, adults who accept the call to be youth leaders want the ability to communicate discipleship and community. But who in our current society knows how to do this? This style of urgent, purposeful ministry is not in vogue in mainline churches. We have forgotten how to ask young persons to lose their lives for the sake of the gospel, to take up their crosses and to follow Jesus Christ. We do not know how to bring a person into the community of faith.

To recover the approach to youth ministry which is able to help young persons be members of the *koinonia*, the leaders must themselves become a core of committed disciples. They must become a team. These leaders will need to meet regularly to study the Bible, pray, share, and learn together. During these meetings and in other ways, the leaders can support, care for, and "stick it out" with one another as a caring, covenanting community. The leaders' meetings include more on the agenda than planning. These meetings are like the "cell" meetings of several generations ago in which a small group of persons committed themselves to one another to engage in regular study, prayer, and mutual support. Out of these experiences of discipleship and community will come the stuff that can be shared with the young persons.

By being committed to one another, the leaders learn how to be committed to the young people. By being the church, the leaders can then share the church with the young people.

Furthermore, in the setting of the *koinonia* the intercessory prayers of the leaders will have their effect.[6] A leader who has prayed for a specific young person may find that his or her own life is changed as a result of that prayer. The intercessory prayer may be uttered in a team meeting or at home, using the youth ministry roster as a prayer list. Or the prayer may be quickly and silently expressed just as a youth activity begins. We cannot trace how God makes prayer effective, for this is an area of mystery and grace. However, as a leader you may discover, for example, that by praying for Robert, bringing Robert before God and asking God to enrich Robert's life, you will begin to see Robert differently. On Sunday night when you encounter Robert at the youth fellowship meeting, he may be seen as a child of God, one for whom Jesus gave his life. Robert may be someone whom Jesus is calling into the community of disciples. Then on Sunday night Robert may act like a fool, albeit a twelve-year-old fool. But how can you say he is a fool, when in your prayers and the prayers of your colleagues, God has taught you that Robert is one whom God loves dearly? Robert has become for you a gift and your life may never be the same.

Leaders are disciples together, ministering to each other. Doing so, they receive the gifts of the Spirit and of community.

These gifts are shared with the young persons, who are brothers and sisters in Christ.

Discipleship, identity, and community are themes which stand as the bedrock for building youth ministry. As adult leaders faithfully and prayerfully infuse each youth ministry activity with these themes, a community of disciples is built up. The hours and efforts expended with young people ultimately are tested by whether or not they will take their places within the community of disciples and devote themselves to active ministry in the world, as servants of the Servant Sovereign Jesus Christ. The biblical passage which most vividly expresses this ideal and which serves as the church's manifesto for its ministry with youth is Ephesians 4:11-16:

> And [Christ's] gifts were that some should be apostles, some prophets, some evangelists, some pastors and teachers, to equip the saints for the work of ministry, for building up the body of Christ, until we all attain to the unity of the faith and of the knowledge of the Son of God, to mature [personhood], to the measure of the stature of the fulness of Christ; so that we may no longer be children, tossed to and fro and carried about with every wind of doctrine, by the cunning of [people], by their craftiness in deceitful wiles. Rather, speaking the truth in love, we are to grow up in every way into him who is the head, into Christ, from whom the whole body, joined and knit together by every joint with which it is supplied, when each part is working properly, makes bodily growth and upbuilds itself in love.

Notes

Chapter 1

[1] Joan Scheff Lipsitz, "Adolescent Development: Myths and Realities," *Children Today* (September-October, 1979), pp. 47-52.

[2] Dietrich Bonhoeffer, *The Cost of Discipleship*. Trans. R. H. Fuller (New York: Macmillan, Inc., 1957). Second edition. © SCM Press Ltd. 1959.

[3] Robert Jay Lifton and Richard Falk, *The Political and Psychological Case Against Nuclearism* (Basic Books, Inc., Publishers, 1982); Robert Jay Lifton, "The Psychic Toll of the Nuclear Age," *The New York Times Magazine* (September 26, 1982), pp. 52-66.

[4] Bonhoeffer, *The Cost of Discipleship*, p. 39.

[5] *Ibid.*, p. 8.

[6] J. B. Phillips, *Letters to Young Churches: A Translation of the New Testament Epistles* (New York: Macmillan, Inc., 1957), p. 341.

Chapter 2

[1] "So You're Growing Up?," *National Lampoon*, 1971. Reprinted with permission of the copyright owner, National Lampoon, Inc.

[2] Joan Scheff Lipsitz, "Adolescent Development: Myths and Realities," *Children Today* (September-October, 1979), pp. 47-52.

[3] *Ibid.*, p. 49.

[4] G. Stanley Hall, *Adolescence: Its Psychology and Its Relation to Physiology, An-*

thropology, Sociology, Sex, Crime, Religion, and Education (New York: Appleton-Century-Crofts, 1904).

[5] Erik H. Erikson, *Childhood and Society* (New York: W. W. Norton & Co. Inc., 1950) Enlarged edition, 1963; see also Erikson, *Identity: Youth and Crisis* (New York: W. W. Norton & Co., Inc., 1968).

[6] Paul B. Irwin, *The Care and Counseling of Youth in the Church* (Philadelphia: Fortress Press, 1975), p. 17. Copyright © 1974 by Fortress Press. Used by permission of Fortress Press.

[7] Lewis J. Sherrill, *The Struggle of the Soul* (New York: Macmillan, Inc., 1951).

[8] Robert J. Lifton, "The Psychic Toll of the Nuclear Age," *The New York Times Magazine* (September 26, 1982), pp. 52-66.

[9] Myron B. Bloy, Jr., "The Young and the Church: Toward a More Serious Piety," *Christianity and Crisis*, vol. 33, no. 13 (July 23, 1973), pp. 143-147.

[10] *Ibid.*, p. 147.

[11] Quoted in Irwin, *The Care and Counseling of Youth*, pp. 44-45. These questions are from Donald McNassor, "Identity Counseling for the Older High School Student," Claremont Graduate School and University Center, 1974.

[12] George I. Bustard, Jr., "The Times That Are Changing—Phase II: The Guarantor," *Strategy: Church Ministry With Youth*, vol. 3, no. 4 (June-August 1973), p. 12.

[13] Dietrich Bonhoeffer, *The Cost of Discipleship*. Trans. R. H. Fuller (New York: Macmillan, Inc., 1957).

[14] *Ibid.*, p. 197.

[15] *Ibid.*, pp. 89-98.

[16] James W. Maddock, "The Future Without History: Youth's Crisis of Commitment," *Religious Education*, vol. LXXI, no. 1 (January-February, 1976). p. 5.

[17] Bonhoeffer, *The Cost of Discipleship*, pp. 15-16.

Chapter 3

[1] Ross Snyder, *Young People and Their Culture* (Nashville: Abingdon Press, 1969), p. 44.

[2] Bill Myers, "Suburbia's High School and the Church," *Religious Education*, vol. LXXII, no. 3 (May-June, 1977), pp. 306-311.

[3] Gwen Kennedy Neville, "Culture, Youth, and Socialization in American Protestantism," in *Religious Education Ministry with Youth*. Edited by D. Campbell Wyckoff and Don Richter (Birmingham: Religious Education Press, 1982).

[4] Dietrich Bonhoeffer, *Life Together*, trans. John W. Doberstein (New York: Harper & Row, Publishers, Inc., 1954).

[5] Specified selections from Bonhoeffer, *Life Together*, p. 110. Reprinted by permission of Harper & Row, Publishers, Inc.

[6] C. Ellis Nelson, *Where Faith Begins* (Atlanta: John Knox Press, 1967), pp. 102-120.

[7] Maria Harris, *Portrait of Youth Ministry* (New York: Paulist Press, 1981), pp. 15-26.

[8] "The Objective of Christian Education for Senior High Young People," The National Council of the Churches of Christ in the U.S.A., 1958.

Chapter 4

[1] Janice M. Corbett, ed., *Explore: Resources for Junior Highs in the Church* (Valley Forge: Judson Press, 1974). This resource and others like it provide back-

ground articles and suggested procedures for adults and young persons to conduct programs dealing with issues relevant to youth.

2 Dietrich Bonhoeffer, *Life Together*, Chapter 4, "Ministry."

3 *Ibid.*, p. 101.

4 *Ibid.*, p. 104.

5 *Ibid.*, p. 108.

6 *Ibid.*, pp. 85-87.